Entrepreneur

startup

Start Your Own

TUTORING &
TEST PREP
BUSINESS

*Your Step-by-Step
Guide to Success*

Entrepreneur Press and Rich Mintzer

**EP
Entrepreneur
Press**

Publisher: Jere L. Calmes
Cover Design: Beth Hansen-Winter
Production and Composition: CWL Publishing Enterprises, Inc., Madison, WI

This publication is designed to provide accurate and authoritative information in regard to the subject matter covered. It is sold with the understanding that the publisher is not engaged in rendering legal, accounting or other professional services. If legal advice or other expert assistance is required, the services of a competent professional person should be sought.

ISBN 13: 978-1-599-918347-3
        10: 1-599-18347-1

Library of Congress Cataloging-in-Publication available.

Printed in Canada
13 12 11 10 09   10 9 8 7 6 5 4 3 2 1

Contents

Chapter 4

Tutoring Business Basics: Location, Structure, and More. **31**

Chapter 5

Money: Finding It, Making It, and Spending It **47**

Chapter 10

Technology and the Tools of the Trade 101

Chapter 11

The Fine Art of Marketing Your Business 111

Chapter 12

Your Sales Strategy

Chapter 13

Other Offerings

Appendix

Tutoring Resources

Preface

Education helps us forge ahead to meet the challenges that await us in the coming years. It is at the core of how we communicate with one another and how we manage in our environment. With that in mind, you, as an entrepreneur, can have a greater purpose (beyond making money) by venturing into the business of education through tutoring and test preparation. In fact, not unlike dedicated teachers, tutors and tutoring business owners take great pride in the accomplishments and successes of their students.

For centuries, children have begrudgingly attended school with a wide variety of outcomes, from honor rolls to dropouts. They have toiled away through class assignments, classroom discussions, pop quizzes, group projects, and far too many homework assignments. They have enlisted their parents' help in a myriad of science projects and brought their trusty #2 pencils to midterms, finals and state, federal, and perhaps even "global" exams. They have been asked to perform, even when under the weather, on entrance exams for private schools, specialized schools and advanced classes, and on university tests that their parents are often more concerned about than they are about attending. They have been haunted by their "permanent records" and cowered in fear of the ominous "report card."

While children may or may not be receptive at first to the idea of adding tutoring to their already mind-expanding school workload, yours is a service that can take the angst out of school.

In the ensuing chapters, we'll look at both the world of tutoring and what it takes to start up a business in general. Of course, hard work and dedication will be part of the plan, as is always the case when starting a business. However, if you are seriously considering becoming an entrepreneur, the tutoring and test prep business is a very enticing venture, one that can be lucrative and rewarding.

Acknowledgments

I'd like to thank Neal Schwartz of Tutoring Club in Armonk, New York; Laurie Hurley of Bright Apple Tutoring in Thousand Oaks, California; Christine D'Amico of ABC-Write Start Read! Inc. in Long Island and New York City; Lynn Giese, president-elect of the National Tutoring Association and head of the tutoring program for Columbus State Community College in Columbus, Ohio; Mark Greenberg of the International Tutoring Association; Andy Sernovitz, author of *Word of Mouth Marketing*; Helen Irlen from the Irlen Institute; Hy Zamft of Zamft Tutoring in Katonah, New York; Eric Stite of the Franchise Business Review; Dave Lipschitz, my brother-in-law, for the usual computer help and the folks at Entrepreneur Media.

Start Your Own

TUTORING &
TEST PREP
BUSINESS

1

An Introduction
to the Tutoring
Business

What Is a Tutoring Business?

Tutoring is defined as assisting a student
with some aspect of his or her schooling and/or testing, which
goes beyond the regular attention provided within the school
environment. While some tutors will freelance and work on
their own, putting up signs and flyers to attract business, the

focus of this book is taking it one step further and actually putting together a business, from your home or from an outside location that provides a number of students with tutors.

From a broad perspective, tutoring is a way of explaining or simplifying schoolwork that the child is either not grasping or is not being taught in an effective manner. It is also a means of encouraging the student to use his or her skills and abilities to their fullest potential. Not unlike a coach, a tutor is most effective when he or she is working with what the student brings to the table and not just teaching randomly in hopes of hitting on that which the student needs to learn.

Over the past five years, tutoring, and the supplemental education market has grown significantly. In fact, it was billed as "an exploding market" by *Newsweek* magazine. As an industry, tutoring passed the $4 billion mark this past year (up 15 percent since 2001) and is continuing to increase in revenues as parents try hard to help their children catch up on schoolwork and prepare for college, which has become increasingly competitive over the past decade.

According to federal government statistics, college enrollment increased by nearly 15 percent from 1980 through 2005 and it's still increasing. And, in case you haven't noticed, there are few new colleges being built to accommodate this increase.

While college preparation is part of the tutoring business, there is a big emphasis on helping children of all ages with challenges from from learning to read to graduating high school and getting into college. An increased awareness of special needs children and those with learning disabilities has also sparked a growing need for specialized learning that schools are generally unable to provide. For these reasons and others listed below, the tutoring industry is clearly growing, with tutoring establishments up from nearly 4,600 tutoring businesses in 2004 to close to 6,000 in 2007, and this does not include the individual tutors. Statistics from the Bureau of Labor Statistics in the U.S. Department of Labor estimate that close to 70,000 people are employed as tutors, not including those who freelance or run a part-time one- or two-person tutoring operation from home.

Why Is There an Increased Need for Tutors?

Looking back 20, 30, or 40 years ago, tutors were helping students much as they are today, (without all the technology, of course). However, if you look back much further, you'll find that as far back as the second century BC, in ancient Greece and ancient Rome, private tutoring was available to the children of the rich who were learning to read and write in Greek and Latin. Thus, the idea is not at all new, but has grown by leaps and bounds, with home, online, and in-class tutoring provided by individuals independently, through small businesses, and through franchised tutoring companies.

Once considered a stigma, the idea of tutoring has become the norm today. The proliferation of tutoring businesses can be largely attributed to several key factors:

- **No Child Left Behind Act:** This federal act, which has come under severe criticism from educational agencies for replacing actual learning with a barrage of testing, has created a situation in which teachers are forced to adhere to a timeline of materials in preparation for statewide tests. Lessons are, therefore, taught at a frantic pace in an effort to keep up with the bombardment of tests that can result in more state funding. In essence, students are being used to help their schools procure more funding since the government has limited money to provide to the schools. The result is that many students either cannot keep up with the pace of the workload or do not test well, meaning they need tutoring to help them catch up and/or help them improve their test-taking skills.

- **Lack of Funding:** As alluded to in the previous paragraph, funding for schools in recent years has slipped down on the American government's list of priorities. In a struggling economy, schools are unable to fund special programs to help students who are falling behind or have special needs.

- **Parents Having Less Available Time:** The increase of two-income families with a wealth of responsibilities (in a struggling economy) has limited the amount of time that many parents have to sit down and review school material or even read with their children.

- **Need for AP Courses:** College used to follow high school. Today, the competition to get into college has created an environment in which high school students need to take advanced placement courses (college-level courses) starting in high school, sometimes as early as ninth or tenth grade. To keep up with these advanced courses and do well in them, students often need tutoring.

- **Competition to Get into College:** As mentioned earlier, getting into college is increasingly difficult as the number of applicants continues to rise at a rate greater than before.

- **Missed Basic Skills:** It's astonishing how many high school graduates still lack many basic math, reading, spelling, and grammar skills. Calculators, spell checkers, and other technologies have minimized the need to learn many basic skills. In addition, because the curriculum is often so packed, many of the basics are taught quickly and without the necessary emphasis. As students get to high school and even college, they find themselves struggling because these skills are often brought into the learning environment, as will also be the case when these students enter the business world. Kids can only get so far without having good basic math and reading skills, and whether it's in high school or afterward, such deficiencies start to catch up with them.

- **Teachers Teaching to the Middle Students:** Most teachers today, with large classes, teach to the middle of the class. Rather than having the opportunity to gear the work to the different academic levels of the students, the schools and the teachers focus on the middle student. The result is that the accelerated students are bored and the struggling students are lost. The result is also that tutors are hired to help challenge students who should be in advanced classes, while helping students on the other end of the curve catch up.

- **Learning Disabilities:** Whether it stems from diet, heredity, broken homes, the media or other heath-related factors, or is possibly the result of advanced means of testing and recognizing the signs and symptoms, there is a marked increased in learning disabilities among students today. Perhaps we are simply paying more attention. Regardless of why, the result is that tutors are needed to help these children with the process of learning and disseminating information.

For these and other reasons, there is a definitive need for tutors at all levels of education. "It doesn't take that much to get lost [in school] these days," says Neal Schwartz, owner of the Tutoring Club in Armonk, New York. "Geometry used to be taught in the ninth grade, now it's taught in eighth grade and some kids are starting on it in the sixth grade. Not only are the kids expected to learn more at a younger grade level, but the testing is like a runaway train. It's at a point where if a teacher wants to get tenure, he or she is going to try to work that much more on packing in the curriculum," adds Schwartz, who also recounts stories of several students coming in for help with social studies. "They got questions wrong on the statewide test because the questions were on the Vietnam War and their class never got up to it. On one hand the teachers can't afford to fall behind. On the other hand, so many students can't keep up," says Schwartz, noting the severity of the problem.

Bright Idea

Make sure you have the coming year's federal and statewide test requirements well in advance of the school year. This will allow you to plan ahead and have tutors ready to help with preparation for these specific exams, while also allowing you to promote your ability to provide help.

How Can You Make a Difference?

There are two ways in which you can make a difference in the tutoring arena. First, you can use your skills as an educator, or as an expert in a particular field, to impart knowledge to students and help them with their schoolwork.

The second approach is starting a tutoring business and serving strictly as the business owner and organizer. In this role, you will be finding, assessing, and hiring skilled tutors while being the entrepreneur.

Of course, there is always the third method, whereby you do both: tutoring on your own and running a business that includes using the abilities of other tutors. These methods are all from the business perspective. From an educational perspective, a tutoring business of any type allows you to make a difference by increasing students' knowledge level and helping students discover and build new skills while improving on those they already have.

Making a difference actually transcends many levels. A successful student–tutor partnership can:

- Bring up the student's test scores and grade average
- Increase the student's overall confidence
- Allow the student to actively participate more in school
- Help the student move into more challenging academic environments
- Help the student get into and achieve success in college and post-graduate studies
- Instill confidence in the student that he or she may not have had in the past

All of these tie into one another. As students see concrete results in the classroom through grades and test scores, they gain overall confidence that leads to greater participation and the confidence to take on greater challenges. In the end, they can achieve greater success in college and beyond.

There is a sense of fulfillment that's hard to match when a tutor sees a marked improvement in a student, especially one who has been struggling. Whether it's learning to read or getting through tenth grade biology, when the light bulb goes on and the student "gets it," the tutor should feel the warmth that comes with a sense of

Beware

Parents often want you to provide specific improvements. Unlike a contractor who will specifically build a new room that measures 12 by 14 feet, you're not in a position to do this when dealing with learning and academic performance, which include so many variables. Therefore, don't let anyone back you into a corner, guaranteeing an "A" or a "90" or any such promises. The best you can do is make it clear that your intentions are to help the student improve his or her grades, score, work habits, learning process, or all of the above. You can, as some tutoring businesses have done, provide a money-back guarantee if the student does not show improvement in x amount of time. But don't make guarantees you may not be able to keep, even with the best of intentions.

accomplishment, and most tutors report that they do. Unlike many jobs, where it's hard to determine the results of your work or see obvious improvement, tutoring has great, clear, rewarding payoffs. Most tutors will tell you stories about students who went from barely passing to passing with honors, or about those who were struggling and then went on to top universities. While tutoring is a way to make money (with little overhead), it's also a way to do something that's constructive, appreciated, and rewarding ... and that counts for something.

Educational Needs of the 21st Century

Interestingly, many educational concerns today are no different than they were decades, or even centuries, ago. Basic reading skills and math skills never go out of style, despite technology. Communications skills, a knowledge of scientific processes and applications, and both world and American history are also still much needed in the 21st century. And then there is technology. As we progress, technical proficiency becomes more significant in the job market. Keeping up with the advances in computers is part of the learning process. Unfortunately, however, it's often mistaken as a substitute for learning. "Why do we have to know that when I can look it up online?" is an all-too-frequent question from young students. While there may be some validity to that question, when it comes to some of the fine points of a subject, there is no doubt that a strong knowledge base, regardless of what the computer can do, is significant for application in other aspects of life.

Today, education also means teaching the benefit of education, which isn't always easy. There are too many shortcuts and many students are drawn to such easy methods of finding quick answers without understanding the concepts behind them. Therefore, one of the primary needs of 21st-century education is to teach and emphasize the importance of learning, storing knowledge, and being able to use the mind as a means of processing information, formulating answers, solving problems, using reasoning skills, and so much more. Technology is a tool that should be used for assistance, not to substitute for these and other, important aspects of learning and knowledge.

Today, unfortunately, thinking is highly underrated.

Stat Fact
Growing competition. In 2005, 16.7 million students enrolled in colleges, a 1.2 million increase over 2000, according to the National Association for College Admission Counseling. That figure is expected to increase another 2.1 million by 2013.

In a Nutshell

A tutoring business is, therefore, a means of putting the right educators with the right students to facilitate learning, whether at the start of school or much farther down the road. Tutors combine their knowledge of subjects with learning techniques to improve the skill level of the students.

To put it into perspective, the modern tutoring business is a service-based business providing a demographic group, or several such groups, with help in one or in several areas of learning. This can be accomplished through the in-person pairing of one-on-one tutors with students, in a classroom setting or by technical means such as over the Internet. The goal is to first assess where the students are academically and then improve their knowledge and ability through the services your business offers.

Like any business, you'll need to determine your target or niche market, find the best location for your business, set up a business plan, determine your finances, and market your services. In the next several chapters, we'll look at the tutoring business specifically and review some of the key overall areas necessary to start up and run a business. There are business basics you'll need to address along with the unique concerns of the tutoring and test prep industry.

2

Do You Have What It Takes?

Anyone deciding to go into his or her own business, whether it means opening a mom-and-pop shop, starting a part-time endeavor, launching a corporation, or buying a franchise, needs to first think about what type of business they want to own and whether they have what it takes to open and run that business. In this case, you need to assess whether tutoring is the right choice and evaluate whether you have the skills necessary to be successful.

No, You Don't Have to Be a Teacher

It is widely thought that the tutoring business is run solely by teachers and education professionals. That's not necessarily the case. Yes, many tutors are teachers or former teachers, but no, to run the business, and even to tutor, it's not a requirement. In fact, many business owners, particularly franchise owners, come from a background in business—often in business management or sales, to be more specific.

"I worked at a large technology company in a number of roles including sales, marketing, and product development," says Neal Schwartz, who wanted less business travel and more time to spend with his family. He took his years of business training and opened the Tutoring Club in Armonk, New York, buying into an established and successful franchise business. Schwartz and other entrepreneurs who come from a background other than education, bring in a variety of business skills and hire the necessary experts as tutors; all while overseeing the business operations. Other owners of tutoring businesses come from various fields.

Laurie Hurley spent 13 years in the hotel industry and several years prior to that in retail management. She then started Bright Apple Tutoring in Thousand Oaks, California. "My experience was working with people and marketing. I was familiar with sales, and that's what I'm doing now—I'm selling a service. When people hear that I'm not a teacher, they ask how I can run this business. That's exactly what it is, a business. I'm managing the flow of my clients and my tutors, it's a lot of work," explains Hurley, who also now sells Home Tutoring Business, which is essentially a "business-in-a-box concept" and another way to get into tutoring. "I've been in this field for a long time, so I thought I would use my background to help other people start home tutoring businesses," explains Hurley, whose business package includes her manual, samples of her fliers, marketing materials, and even Yellow Pages ads, plus a CD and a variety of forms that she uses on a regular basis. "I offer a consultation with me by phone and/or e-mail, and if they need more they can have additional hours, but I charge an hourly rate for those," explains Hurley.

Those who do come from the teaching profession may approach the business from the opposite direction, supplying the tutoring skills and then building a business around their own expertise. "I'm a reading specialist with 18 years' experience teaching in the New York City school system," says Christine D'Amico, president of ABC-Write Start Read! Inc. For D'Amico, the tutoring business, in Long Island and New York City, grew from her own individual tutoring. "What happened was that I got too many clients for myself and had to hire people to handle the extra work," says D'Amico, who trains each of her tutors in the methods she uses. "I know about a variety of available programs that I've researched. My main focus is to provide a really good product. I know what they're (the students) getting from the school system and what they're not getting," adds D'Amico, who tries to fill those gaps with her tutoring service.

These are the three most popular approaches to the tutoring business, each of which can be effective:

- Use your own educational background and expertise to start a business.
- Use your own business background to start a business and employ tutors.
- Use your own business or educational background and buy a tutoring franchise.

Necessary Skills

Be forewarned: you can be an expert in math or science, but not launch a successful tutoring business based on those skills alone. Many excellent educators run into all sorts of difficulties because they do not possess some of the other skills necessary to run this type of business successfully. You need to combine expertise with a variety of business skills if you're coming from an education background. Even if you're a one-person operation, you need to be good at scheduling, communicating effectively with people (especially parents), marketing yourself, record keeping, and pricing your services.

While reading the next few sections, you can evaluate which skills you possess, which ones you need to hone, and which may be best left to someone else to handle. Remember, good entrepreneurs know their own strengths and, rather than trying to "fudge" areas in which they have weaknesses, bring in competent help. Therefore, you may look for business associates or employees who can help you in certain areas. For example, you may have a knack for scheduling, balancing the budget, and finding the best facility for your needs, and may even have some tech abilities. However, you may not be comfortable making hiring decisions on your own. So, what can you do? Bring in a consultant in human resources who can help you find and evaluate tutors. Likewise, if you're a great people person, but lack confidence in your bookkeeping and budgeting abilities, you would call on someone with the accounting skills to help you get your books in order and set up (and stick to a budget). Again, this can be someone with whom you work a few days each month, rather than a full-timer … at least until your business grows to a point where you need someone to handle these functions on a full-time basis. Remember, a good entrepreneur knows his or her strengths and weaknesses and compensates accordingly.

Stat Fact

If you're wondering if anyone is making money in the tutoring and test preparation industry, consider that in 2005, total payroll wages were reported at just under $1 billion and through 2007, they had grown to $1.2 billion.

Are You Good at Scheduling?

Are you diligent about maintaining an up-to-date calendar of appointments, meetings, and upcoming engagements? Are you often organizing and reorganizing your schedule, or do you jot things down on slips of paper and have to search for them to remember where you need to be and when?

Neal Schwartz considers scheduling the toughest part of running a tutoring business. It's not hard to understand why, if you spend an hour in his office and listen to phone calls coming in canceling or asking to change appointments, mostly at short notice. Locking in available times for tutors, most of whom have day jobs (or may be college students) is only half the battle. The other half is trying to coordinate times for students, who also have soccer practice, piano lessons, karate classes, after-school activities, and, if they are older, jobs, not to mention other homework. If your tutors are doing at-home tutoring, you also need to factor travel time into the schedule. If you have a tutoring facility, you need to determine how many students you can accommodate at any one given time and not "overbook" your space. The trick is to have each area designated for tutoring occupied at all hours that you are open. Therefore, if you're open from 3 p.m. until 8 p.m. each school day and can accommodate seven students at any given time in quiet areas or cubicles, then you want to have 35 scheduled students, or seven for each of the five hours. This, of course, means that your scheduled tutors are also available. Good luck completing this seemingly simple task. Filling 28 of the 35 slots would be considered very good, considering cancellations.

Software programs can help you move appointments around and maintain a clear view of what is scheduled for any given hour, but they can't help you when a parent calls to cancel a session an hour in advance or when three people "need" the same time slot. If you don't possess (or aren't ready to learn) good scheduling skills, then you will probably have a difficult time in the tutoring business.

Are You a People Person?

Yes, tutors need people skills to work effectively with students. *But*, you also need excellent people skills to run such a business. While nobody says you need an outgoing, bubbly personality, you do need good, professional interpersonal skills and to be able to open up clear lines of communication. You will typically be interacting with:

- Tutors
- Students
- Suppliers and vendors
- Teachers
- Parents

Customer service is not typically thought of as part of tutoring. Typically the focus is on how well the tutor knows the subject and whether he or she can help the student learn. While that is one of the most basic aspects of the tutoring process, you also need to remember that you're in the service business, which means attracting business, providing an overview of what you offer, setting up a mutually agreeable time and place for rendering such services, getting payment for services, and accumulating repeat customers. The only way to do this effectively is by communicating well with all the people in this circle and handling problems, complaints, and concerns professionally and courteously. Yes, customer service applies, meaning you need to be flexible but firm enough not to allow tutors or clients to take advantage of you.

Throughout the upcoming sections we'll talk about your relationship with tutors and evaluating students. One relationship that will always be important is that with parents. After all, they are your clients, since they are typically footing the bill for tutoring or test prep. Whether you're comfortable with parents can be the telltale sign as to whether you're going into the right business.

Can You Withstand the Parents?

Consider the following telephone conversation between the owner of a tutoring facility and a parent of one of the students.

Parent: Hi, I want to know how my daughter is doing.

Owner: Well, she's only been here twice, so we really don't have a lot of data.

Parent: Do you think she's stupid?

Owner: No, I really don't think she's stupid. I just think that she's very far behind.

Parent: Well, how did she get so far behind?

Owner: Well, I really don't know what happened at school because I wasn't there to observe it, but she's fallen behind in her work.

Parent: What do you mean?

Owner: I mean that we'll work with her to catch her up to where she should be.

Parent: Why is she behind?

Owner: As I said, I'm not in the classroom, so I can't tell you for sure.

Parent: Do you think she's stupid?

If this type of interaction doesn't scare you away, then perhaps you're on the right track.

While parents have the best intentions, they often aren't carrying around realistic pictures of their children, except perhaps in their wallets. You are therefore dealing with individuals who can be unrealistic in their expectations of the child, the tutor, the teachers, or the entire educational system. Rarely is it ever the fault of the parent who signed his or her child up for music lessons, Little League, and swimming lessons, while still expecting the child to get homework done on time and do a fair amount of studying. Few parents step back and take a realistic look at the situation without looking for blame. Often the problem is compounded by parents failing to recognize their sons' and daughters' improvement or seeking grades that aren't realistic. Parents should encourage their children to do their best, try to facilitate learning as a positive thing, and reward children for their efforts. They should work with the tutors to get results rather than presenting a "Well, what can you do for us?" attitude.

Remember, your job as a business owner depends largely on good customer relations, and since the parents are the ones paying for the tutoring, they are the customers. You need patience and diplomacy when dealing with a parent who insists that his or her child should be taught in a particular manner or complains because the child is not making immediately measurable progress.

The best that you can do is make necessary and reasonable accommodations while standing behind the system that you've established. In other words, be flexible, work within the framework of what you have available, and don't let yourself be bullied. If it's a matter of switching tutors, that may provide the answer. If it's a matter of switching times, that may also be helpful. However, if it's a matter of doing the child's homework for them, you may need to politely explain that your tutors don't do that; they will help, guide, or teach, but they don't actually *do* the work for the students.

To make your job easier, you should have literature available in advance explaining how your tutoring system works. For example, is it one-on-one tutoring in your facility where the tutor first assesses the needs of the student and then works on areas in which the student needs help? Is it a specific set manner in which you approach reading or math or another subject? Also explain that learning takes time, improvement is an incremental thing, and pressure does not typically facilitate the learning process. You can also let parents know that your business and your tutors are working to create a supportive environment, if that is the case. The point is, whatever your approach is, lay it out on the table ahead of time. Then have parents sign that they have read your literature.

Can You Hire and Fire?

Unless you're planning to do this on your own, which is freelancing, rather than forming a full tutoring business, you'll need to learn how to hire, and in some cases fire, tutors. In actuality, you're not usually hiring tutors on an "employee" basis, but instead are using a group of freelancers or independent contractors who will work as part of your tutoring business, representing your company, but not on a salaried basis. In some instances, such as that of the Tutoring Club, tutors use various methodologies when teaching, based on the principle of focusing on areas within the subject that the students do not know. In other instances, such as that of Christine D'Amico, tutors are taught a specific methodology that has been proven to work. We will discuss the different styles of learning later. For now, we return to the question: Can you screen and take on people who you feel will be good tutors for your business and let go of people who you believe aren't doing the job properly or aren't representing your tutoring business in a positive manner?

Hiring tutors means finding and assessing the skills and abilities of people who have expertise or strength in a certain area and can relay their knowledge effectively to students. "I've always found that you want to go with people's strengths. When you try to move someone out of their area of strength, that's where you can run into problems," says Neal Schwartz, who has found that even people who are strong in a subject don't necessarily make good tutors. The fact is that while you want to look for reputable individuals with excellent resumes and references, you cannot tell for sure if a person will make a good tutor until he or she works with students.

Besides finding people with expertise in specific areas of education, you want to find tutors who:

- Can commit to a regular schedule, even if it's a few hours a week.
- Have clean backgrounds regarding drugs, problems with the law, etc.
- Have good communications skills, including the ability to listen. Someone may have a strong knowledge of the subject matter, but if the student is asking questions, or telling the tutor that he or she doesn't understand something, the tutor must hear that and provide the necessary help.
- Treat students and parents professionally and with respect, and never be condescending.
- Be flexible, caring individuals with patience.
- Understand that children (and adults) learn in various manners and not all at the same pace.
- Enhance and not damage the reputation of your business.

Later in the book, we will include more on what you should expect from your tutors. For now, it's important that you know what you're looking for and are able to evaluate the people who will be working for you. It's a combination of expertise, personality, communication skills, and professionalism that makes for a good tutor. You need to be able to assess these qualities.

You also need to be able to do damage control when a tutor fails to show up, does not act in a responsible manner, or is rude or disrespectful to a client. Business owners have spent out-of-pocket expenses to pay another tutor to take over, free of charge, and go to the client for at least one or two sessions to make up for such poor conduct on the part of a tutor. You will need to be able to differentiate between a misunderstanding or an unfortunate incident and when someone simply cannot do the job effectively. "We had one tutor who was very bright, but her manner, her body language, and the way in which she presented herself were very off-putting to the students, so we had to let her go," explains Neal Schwartz.

You will also need to be able to work with a lot of tutors, since many will come and go as your business grows. "I usually have three times as many tutors as we can have here at any one time," adds Schwartz, whose business runs from a facility rather than at clients' homes. For Hurley, there are some 60–70 tutors on her list. She knows this is an industry with some degree of turnover, since tutors are typically part-timers. Some will relocate, while others may find that they don't have the same amount of time that they used to have. Still others simply get burned out.

Putting It All Together

Years ago, matchmakers looked long and hard to find the right pairing of husband and wife. If they could find match several couples in the course of a year they were highly rewarded. Today, there are many businesses that pair up people for various purposes from dating services to roommate locators to cleaning services, nanny services, and tutoring services. One of your key skills as a business owner in this industry is being able to match up a student with a tutor who understands the needs of the specific student and can meet the challenges of teaching and/or explaining material to that student. In making such a match you'll need to consider personalities as well as skills. "I meet with the parent and children before I send a tutor to any home," says Hurley, who wants to make the right match. "I look for a tutor who I feel will connect with the student," says Schwartz, who is also ready to make a change of tutors if the student isn't showing improvement.

You may use testing or other means of assessing the student. Be careful, however, as tests may not show the specific problems. In some cases, the student simply doesn't perform well on a test, but does know the material. For many tutoring businesses, assessments are a combination of talking with the parent and child as well as reviewing what the child has been doing in school. This can be done by looking at recent homework assignments, recent quizzes, and tests, and even talking with the child's teacher(s).

Bright Idea

Look for certified tutors. You can seek certified tutors through one of several tutoring associations. The National, American, and International Tutoring Associations all provide such certifications. In fact the ITA offers freelance tutors a means of getting certification for $60 or less.

In addition, as a business owner, you serve as much more than a matchmaker, since you are in charge of maintaining the schedules, finding quality tutors, marketing your business, and handling paperwork, payment, and taxes. Your business is responsible for making a difference and your tutors are responsible for upholding your reputation for educating students.

There are many levels at which you can approach this business. The point is, you can serve as a tutor yourself and have a few other tutors who handle your overflow, you can have a small home-based business with a dozen tutors, or you can have a major business with 200 clients and 60 or more tutors. The key will be how well you're able to handle the task of putting together students and tutors in appropriate environments within specific schedules. As Laurie Hurley says, "It's a difficult business, but you can get into the flow of it."

Another business option is to become a facilitator, taking on the role of matchmaker. This type of business pairs freelance tutors in one or several areas with students seeking tutors. You don't do the training, nor do you set up the times for the student and tutor to meet. Tutors pay to be listed and you make matches based on the subjects and other criteria you want to include. Of course, the tutors should have good credentials and/or certification or your reputation for making quality matches will suffer. The internet has allowed this type of tutoring facilitation business to reach a broader market than ever before. Of course, you'll still need to handle marketing and have good online skills to make this work. The people at TutorNation.com have had great success at such tutor–student matching. They also offer tips for tutoring, plus access to ITA certification from their website.

Do You Have What It Takes?

Here's a short quiz. Rate yourself 1–10 (be honest), 10 being the highest:

I'm good at making and sticking to a schedule. ____

I'm comfortable making last-minute changes. ____

I'm a good judge of character. ____

I'm comfortable communicating with a wide range of people. ____

I consider myself a patient person. ____

It takes a lot for me to lose my cool. ____

I'm good at multitasking. ____

If you add up your totals and you score over 45, then you're a strong candidate to take on a tutoring business.

Know Your
Market

Before you embark on any business venture, you need to know what it is that you plan to sell and who it is that will buy your product or service. These two important considerations go hand in hand. They're usually dependent on one another. For example, if you have expertise in a particular area of education, such as teaching reading to young, new readers, you'll have a service to present and your target market will be mothers (and fathers) of young children. Conversely, if you plan to open a tutoring business and will be hiring tutors to help first- through 12th-grade students in several areas, including math, science, and English, you can look at a broader market and focus on a target group of parents whose children are falling behind in any of these areas. No matter what you hope to sell, whether it's strictly tutoring, test preparation, or both, you'll need to determine whether there's a significant piece of the pie in whichever geographic location you choose. And, if you are web-based, you'll need to determine whether you're offering the much broader web community something it can use, again finding a target market.

Beware

Too many business owners assume that because the internet is so wide reaching, they will inevitably draw a large consumer market. In reality this isn't the case. In the early days of the internet boom, everyone was putting up websites expecting great things, much like the 300 brands of automobiles that existed when the automobile first hit the market in the early 1900s. In time, however, just like the automobile industry boiled down to the few major brands that would survive, the internet followed the same path. In 2000 at an Internet trade show, there were all sorts of online auction sites, one of which let you bid on several auction sites at once. The problem was that eBay soon blew most of this vast number of competitors out of the water. In fact, can you name another online auction site off the top of your head? Exactly. So don't assume that yet another online tutoring site will assure your success. You need to do something unique and draw a target audience ... even online.

Researching the Market

A tutoring business will only survive if there's a need for such a service. In a senior community, you won't likely find many students, while in a community with numerous families, you're more likely to find children who need help with their schoolwork. Of course, researching the market is a bit more complicated and will be discussed later when we talk about marketing, promotion, and advertising in Chapter 11.

To begin with, you'll be looking at specific geographic areas in which you could logically and realistically open a business. This means factoring in your travel time, the cost of running a business from a location, or the potential of running a business from your home. You'll want to look at the market in any potential neighborhood and determine whether it's over-served or underserved. Numerous tutoring services in a small town may mean there won't be a large enough slice of the pie for you to cash in on. You'll need to consider the overall population and the number of potential clients (students), and see if there is room for another tutoring business to set up shop. Perhaps there are several college test prep businesses, but nothing serving the often underserved middle school community. Perhaps in a college town, there is a great population of students and not enough extra services for them. If you can fill that niche, or any particular niche, then you can make a go of it.

Look at the area demographics to see if there's a large enough student population to make a tutoring business worth exploring. Also scout local competition carefully when evaluating a neighborhood. Call some of the tutoring businesses or even private tutors advertising in supermarkets and elsewhere to find out how much they charge and how far they travel if they do in-home tutoring. Pick a location that's a little bit out of town and see if they serve that neighborhood as well. Pose as a potential customer and see what other businesses offer.

Bright Idea

Call a tutoring center on behalf of three children of different ages and inquire if the center has tutoring at their different levels. Find out what kinds of tutoring and the costs. One of your young students should be entering his or her junior year of high school so you can ask about SAT preparation.

You'll want to find out the overall number of students in a given area. The International Center for Education Statistics (nces.ed.gov) and School Matters (schoolmatters.com) can be helpful in your search for school demographic information.

Look for your audience. For example, if you plan to tutor young readers, then you need to find out the population of young children attending schools in your area. If, however, you're looking to set up an SAT preparation course, then you're looking at the number of high school students. If you have not yet determined which grade levels you will focus on, then you'll want to look at the numbers across the board and determine how many total students attend school in the area.

You can also look at the academic success of the schools. Are they posting high academic scores, or are students struggling? What percentage of students goes on to college? There are websites and data available in local libraries that can help you in your search. You can also contact the schools and ask to speak to a guidance counselor. You'll get a mixed reaction. Some won't be interested and some won't have the time to talk with you, while others will be happy to let you know that there are plenty of students who could use your services. Reading local newspapers is another way to catch up on how the schools are faring. Some have local funding for after-school programs, while many do not. By combining primary research, including asking parents and teachers for information, and secondary research from books and periodicals, you can find a lot of information about the market you plan to enter.

When you talk to parents, you can discuss the educational issues and concerns in the area. Be straightforward and ask if they feel tutoring could be helpful. In fact, you might create a questionnaire asking if they would seek tutoring for their children. Offer a few possible price ranges.

While researching the educational needs of the area and all possible competition, you'll also need to assess whether a neighborhood can afford your services. Not that you will necessarily have a set price, but you will want to gauge the likelihood that parents will be able to afford $50 a week for perhaps 20 weeks, or $1,000, for a tutor for their child.

The end result of your market research will be a yea or nay for a given area or neighborhood based on:

- The number of potential clients
- The competition in the area
- The likelihood that parents will be able to afford your service
- The potential to make a profit after covering your expenses

Niche Markets

Almost every business has at least one, if not several, niche markets. These smaller pieces of the overall pie provide opportunities for entrepreneurs to reach a smaller segment of the market with more specialized products or services. It also allows you, as a business owner, to focus more heavily on advertising to a core group.

In the tutoring business, you'll need to first determine which, if any, niche markets are underserved and which ones, if any, are those in which you have expertise. If you don't have the expertise, these will be the areas in which you will look for tutors.

Below are some of the niche markets within the larger tutoring and test prep market.

Reading Tutors

It's no secret that learning to read is the cornerstone of education. With that in mind, there are many tutors who work with young readers, typically ages five and up, to help with their reading skills. Most often a tutor helps facilitate the process and can benefit students who are having trouble with early reading skills. Tutors need to know effective reading development strategies and skills that support developing literacy. This can include work with phonics, vocabulary development, constructing words with magnetic letters or blocks, and other reading programs. Such tutors need to be well versed in child-friendly communications.

"I'm a reading specialist with a lot of credentials and have been teaching for 18 years, so I started my tutoring business based on my own expertise," says Christine

D'Amico, who started ABC-Write Start Read! "I know about a variety of available programs that I've researched," she adds.

While some parents are determined to create baby geniuses by trying to teach their toddlers to read, it's not yet proven that toddler tutoring can be effective. In fact, Maryanne Wolf, head of Tufts University's Center for Reading and Language Research, was quoted in late 2007 stating the following: "Recent brain-imaging data show that children aren't ready to read until around age 5 at the earliest. To hasten that process not only makes no sense socially or emotionally, it makes no sense physiologically."

Reading tutors and bringing in reading "specialists" are discussed further in Chapter 12, on other options you can offer.

Middle School Tutoring

A wide open and broad-based market, tutoring in this area ranges from comprehension and skills development to help keeping up with the often-hurried curriculum and tackling homework issues. While some parents give too much credence strictly to grades, the goals at this juncture should be an understanding of the subjects and developing broad-based skills such as problem solving, reasoning, and overall writing proficiency. After all, while parents should want their children to get good grades, the reality is that no one ever looks at middle school grades unless the child is applying to a specialized high school. Therefore, re-training parents to focus in part on grades and in part on preparedness for high school (where grades are more important) can be part of your approach.

Tutoring students in grades six through eight is largely about teaching them how to stay focused amid the many distractions vying for their attention, especially as puberty strikes. Finding tutors who know how to communicate well with this often-neglected age group is essential and can be a lucrative market.

Having access to the school curriculum is also important. "I know the curriculum because I'm in the schools," says Christine D'Amico of ABC-Write Start Read!

High School Tutoring

At the high school level, a tutor is typically brought in when a student is falling behind or struggling to pass a course or several courses. Grades matter for college admissions and tutors at this level are typically using new means of explaining information to students who aren't getting it. In some cases, tutors are also helping students who are in advanced classes and college-level courses to stay "ahead of the curve."

Many high schools today offer peer tutoring programs. In these programs, students with greater academic proficiency help students who are behind in their class work. In some instances this works well, while in other situations the students' personalities don't click, or students are embarrassed to work with a peer. From a business standpoint, you need to research such peer tutoring programs in your area to determine what you can offer. You may be able to offer training for the high school tutors or, if such programs are underused, offer standard tutoring services. Again, you need tutors who can relate well to high school students.

College Preparation and Test Prep

College preparation is typically a separate business that can mean serving as a college planning consultant who helps with everything from making the necessary grades, to choosing the right college and filling out the paperwork, to some basic guidance on how to select a college.

Test preparation, however, means getting students ready for college entrance examinations, most notably the SAT or the ACT. While tutoring businesses more commonly feature one-to-one scenarios, test prep is often provided in classroom settings. Most tutoring businesses also engage in the test preparation business, and why not? It's a $400 million industry with students flocking to receive help on the daunting exams that in the past decade have become more significant than ever in college admissions.

Often SAT and ACT prep courses are taught by teachers or former teachers who have studied the methods of prepar-

Stat Fact
Research by the College Board, the administrators of the SAT, found that students can increase their scores about 40 points by taking the exam a second time after taking a short SAT prep course.

ing for and performing well on the tests and have their own approach to taking them. We'll look more at the test prep part of your business in Chapter 8.

Homeschool Tutoring

In the past 10 years, there has been a steady increase in the number of children being homeschooled in the United States. There are certainly a number of arguments on both sides, some touting the potential to focus on learning and education through homeschooling, rather than teaching toward standardized tests, while opposing arguments point out the lack of socialization and exposure to diverse cultures and backgrounds. Arguments for and against homeschooling notwithstanding, tutors can play a role in accentuating the learning experience.

If you're unfamiliar with homeschooling, and the state laws in particular, you may want to visit Homeschool Central online at homeschoolcentral.com, a comprehensive website where you'll find a wealth of information on homeschooling. Your state department of education can also fill you in on the laws.

From a tutoring perspective, you are offering help for parents who are homeschooling their children, which means your tutors are there to support the ongoing curriculum as introduced by the parent(s). It's not the job of the tutor to introduce new learning strategies or techniques unless discussed first with the parents, nor is it the tutor's job to discuss the merits or shortcomings of homeschooling.

Typically, the curriculum falls into one of several categories, which include:

- Working directly from textbooks and/or workbooks
- Using computer-based CD-ROMs and online lesson plans
- Literature-based learning
- An eclectic mix, bringing together a combination of learning styles.

Of course, these are broad learning categories, and homeschooled children can certainly benefit from their parents' awareness of how they best learn.

Much as tutors need to familiarize themselves with the school curriculum in their region or community, homeschool tutors need to familiarize themselves with the homeschool curriculum being used in the specific home and know what level the student has achieved to date.

Typically, parents who are homeschooling their children will turn to a tutor for help in a subject or subjects that they are not confident in their abilities to teach. Since children are often learning quickly in this one-on-one learning situation, the fast pace can sometimes cause a need for the parent to call in outside assistance from someone with expertise in the particular area. In some cases, the tutor is also asked to guide the parent in upcoming lessons on a difficult topic. It's therefore important to discuss in advance the subject or subjects in which the parent and student require a tutor, not unlike meeting with parents and students to initiate any type of tutoring.

Rates should be similar to those for any other home tutoring offered, set up by the hour. The primary difference between tutoring students from schools and tutoring students who are learning from home is that the tutor needs to be filled in on the curriculum and the progress to date.

Children with Learning Disabilities

If you discover an underserved population of students with learning disabilities, you can start a business that focuses on this important niche market. Of course, you'll need to hire tutors who have special training working in this market, whether it's with ADD and ADHD students or those with dyslexia, autism, or any other special issue or disability.

Many tutoring businesses cater to several of these demographic markets, hiring highly trained tutors who are comfortable (and capable) working with learning-disabled students of different ages and educational backgrounds. Researching the market in a given community will provide insight into which areas you should focus on, and in some cases, which niche market you should emphasize.

Keep in mind that while seeking a niche market, if you're coming to tutoring with experience in a certain area, you can use that as a starting point and branch out from there. Christine D'Amico started ABC-Write Start Read! as primarily a tutoring service providing reading help, based on her background and expertise. However, the business expanded to math, science, and other subjects.

The Market for Tutors

Along with finding clients, it will be necessary to determine how many independent tutors are marketing their services and the number of competitive businesses using tutors in a given area. In some areas, there's a large population of both former and currently employed teachers who can be valuable as tutors.

Unless you're setting up an online tutoring service, which we'll discuss later, you'll want the tutors you hire to be close to either your business or the homes of the clients, depending on how your business is set up. Put some feelers out before launching your business and see how many bites you get. Run an ad looking for tutors and see if you get a good response. Ask around and see if you find receptive potential tutors in the neighborhood.

Costs and Profits

The other important factor to take into consideration when doing your market research is whether you can make money with a tutoring business in a particular community. "Like any other business, when you do your marketing evaluation, you'll want to determine whether or not the community can support another tutoring business and, if so, how much can your tutors earn per hour and how much can you make," says Lynn Giese, president-elect of the National Tutoring Association and head of the tutoring program for Columbus State Community College in Columbus, Ohio. You'll need to check out your competition and the economic climate of the area to determine if you'll be able to make a living after paying your expenses. Of course, you'll also need to determine the type of tutoring operation you'll be able to handle. For example, with the low overhead of a homebased tutoring business with tutors going to the homes of students, you might be able to make a go of it in an area where leasing space for on-location tutoring would be too costly.

This will require economic market research and, of course, punching in some

Stat Fact
It's estimated that the cost to hire a private tutor in the United States typically ranges from $25 to $150 per hour, depending on the area of the country and what the tutor is doing.

numbers with your accountant. More on startup costs and the expenses of running a tutoring business will come up later.

Green Tutoring

All businesses today are making a conscious effort to be greener, or at least they should be. While your CO_2 output should not be especially high from a tutoring business, especially if it's homebased, there are several green-minded ways in which you can launch and run your business.

For starters, be aware of your paper needs and try to minimize them as much as possible. Printing on two sides of a page is a start and e-mailing what does not need to be printed is an even better way of saving paper. Sharing a central printer obviously saves more energy than having five or six printers all running at once. You can also use recycled products, including paper and even computer cartridges. Reusing materials is another way to be environmentally conscious. A fresh coat of non-toxic paint can spruce up old tables or chairs for future use, provided they are safe. Always look for uses before discarding furniture or even equipment.

Alternate means of transportation are another way to save energy. Tutors can bike to nearby sessions or to and from the tutoring facility, or if some live nearby, they can take a few extra minutes and walk. You can consider ridesharing or carpooling if several tutors are all coming in for the same hours from a nearby location.

You can also save energy by making sure computers are turned off for the evening. Use lighting that features the LED or CRT bulbs that are longer-lasting and more energy-efficient than incandescent bulbs. Likewise, energy-efficient equipment with the Energy Star seal should also be high on your list of machinery to buy. Renewable energy sources, such as wind and solar power, are worth considering when scouting out your location, or even for your home. You'll need to look at the current costs associated with such alternate means of energy and then look at the cost savings down the road, which will usually be substantial. The question for most new businesses is whether the startup money is available to start off with green energy. In many cases, businesses start with a percentage of their facility (or even your home) switching to renewable energy.

Ultimately, if you can run your business in a manner that is as close to carbon-neutral as possible, you'll benefit the planet and also show your clients, as well as the community, that you're taking a stand in the vitally important environmental arena.

State Standards

It's essential for any tutoring facility to be aware of the requirements of the state, or states, in which they do business.

While the federal government has overall guidelines in place for education, such as No Child Left Behind, which has been met with mixed reviews, the standards for education are set by each of the 50 states, plus the District of Columbia. Requirements for meeting state standards to move on to the next grade level and for high school graduation are determined by the department of education in each state and should be reviewed carefully before you start a tutoring business in a given state. For online tutoring, you'll need to either work on general principles, homework, or lessons only, or be aware of the needs for each state. In any event, you should have access to such information.

State requirements are always subject to change and with that in mind, you should keep up with the latest rules and requirements set forth by specific states. Here is a state-by-state online directory of department of education websites. Look at the requirements for the grade levels and make sure you have copies of the necessary tests.

Alabama Department of Education: **alsde.edu**

Alaska Department of Education & Early Development: **eed.state.ak.us**

Arizona Department of Education: **ade.state.az.us**

Arkansas Department of Education: **arkansased.org**

California Department of Education: **cde.ca.gov**

Colorado Department of Education: **cde.state.co.us**

Connecticut State Department of Education: **sde.ct.gov/sde/site/default.asp**

Delaware Department of Education: **doe.state.de.us**

District of Columbia Public School System: **k12.dc.us**

Florida Department of Education: **fldoe.org**

Georgia Department of Education: **doe.k12.ga.us**

Hawaii Department of Education: **doe.k12.hi.us**

Idaho State Department of Education: **sde.idaho.gov**

Illinois State Board of Education: **isbe.state.il.us**

Indiana Department of Education: **doe.state.in.us**

Iowa Department of Education: **iowa.gov/educate**

Kansas State Department of Education: **ksde.org**

Kentucky Department of Education: **kde.state.ky.us**

Louisiana Department of Education: **doe.state.la.us**

Maine Department of Education: **state.me.us/education**

Maryland State Department of Education: **marylandpublicschools.org/msde**

Massachusetts Department of Education: **doe.mass.edu**

Michigan Department of Education: **michigan.gov**

Minnesota Department of Education: **education.state.mn.us**

Missouri Department of Elementary & Secondary Education: **dese.mo.gov**

Montana Office of Public Education: **opi.state.mt.us**

Nebraska Department of Education: **nde.state.ne.us**

Nevada Department of Education: **nde.doe.nv.gov**

New Hampshire Department of Education: **ed.state.nh.us**

New Jersey Department of Education: **state.nj.us**

New Mexico Public Education Department: **sde.state.nm.us**

New York State Education Department: **emsc.nysed.gov**

North Carolina State Board of Education: **ncpublicschools.org**

North Dakota Department of Public Instruction: **dpi.state.nd.us**

Ohio Department of Education: **ode.state.oh.us**

Oklahoma State Department of Education: **sde.state.ok.us**

Oregon Department of Education: **ode.state.or.us**

Pennsylvania Department of Education: **pde.state.pa.us**

Rhode Island Department of Education: **ride.ri.gov**

South Carolina Department of Education: **ed.sc.gov**

South Dakota Department of Education: **doe.sd.gov**

Tennessee Department of Education: **tennessee.gov/education**

Texas Education Agency: **tea.state.tx.us**

Utah State Office of Education: **usoe.k12.ut.us**

Vermont Department of Education: **education.vermont.gov**

Virginia Department of Education: **doe.virginia.gov**

Washington Office of Superintendent of Public Instruction: **k12.wa.us**

West Virginia Department of Education: **wvde.state.wv.us**

Wisconsin Department of Public Instruction: **dpi.wi.gov**

Wyoming Department of Education: **k12.wy.us**

Once you're aware of the state standards and requirements, make sure to update your tutors on this information. Also, let parents know that you're working toward meeting these standards.

Tutoring Business
Basics: Location, Structure, and More

While setting up your tutoring business, there are a number of basics you'll need to consider, some of which are industry-specific, while others are germane to all new businesses. To begin, you'll want to think through each concern before making any decisions and, in fact, possibly call in some experts for advice, including your accountant and a business attorney. Your decisions should be predicated by:

1. The size and scope of the business you're looking to open. Will you be running a tutoring business as a part-time side business or are you setting up a full-time enterprise? Are you hoping to start and maintain a small business with five to 10 tutors, or hoping to start a major business that will eventually have several locations?

2. The amount of money you're looking to make and whether you can reach your goals in a given neighborhood (remember, you should have already done your market research). Are you looking to make a comfortable income for yourself and your family, or launch a million-dollar corporation?

3. The type of tutoring and/or test prep business you're looking to open. Will you work from a specific onsite tutoring location? Will you operate a homebased business? An online business?

Location

Your location will depend largely on the type of business you're looking to open and the services offered. For example, if you're sending tutors to the homes of students, you'll need only a small office, which you can set up in your home. If you're holding test prep classes, you'll need a facility with classroom space. Following are some pros and cons of each.

Homebased Tutoring

Many successful tutoring businesses have a homebased location, while sending tutors to the homes of students. Often tutors independently handle this kind of freelance tutoring service on their own. However, by launching such a business you can provide the organization, marketing, and scheduling, and lend credibility by having a company name. You can also offer training for tutors so they can charge more.

While a homebased business refers to running the business from your home, homebased tutoring refers to tutoring in the student's home, both of which are manners of running such a business with lower costs.

Laurie Hurley, who owns Bright Apple Tutoring, Accounting Tools for Tutors (her software business), and Home Tutoring Business, from which she sells tutoring packages to entrepreneurs starting out, has always run her businesses from a home location. "I started in a hallway in my home," says Hurley. "I had a desk and everybody was walking by all the time. At that time it was just my husband and our first child. I worked from the dining room, the living room, and finally now have my own room with a door. But I would never rent office space, not when you can save on overhead by working from home," says Hurley. As is typically the case with working from home, you'll want to find a location in your house that:

- Has few distractions
- Is easily accessible to the outside if tutors or clients are meeting you there (so they don't have to walk through your entire house)
- Has the necessary outlets for your office equipment and room for storage
- Has good ventilation and good lighting
- Is a place in which you can feel comfortable doing your work

While the positive side of running your business from home is obviously the low overhead costs, the drawback can be meeting tutors and students. You can certainly invite tutors to your home for initial meetings and training if you have enough space and some quiet time. However, it's less practical to have students and parents showing up at your door on a regular basis. You will, therefore, need to screen students via telephone or, as Laurie Hurley does, visit the homes of all potential clients to meet the parents and children. "I'll never send a tutor to work with someone that I haven't met first," says Hurley.

Another popular option is to find a location, such as a school or library, that will allow you to use a room for such meetings and/or training sessions, possibly for a nominal fee. This eliminates the ongoing costs of an office, while providing a place outside of your home in which to conduct business with others.

If you do go with an office outside of your home, you can look for a relatively small space. Location will be a greater factor if people are coming to meet with you, as opposed to you going to their homes or screening by phone. Again, you'll need to decide in advance how you'll handle the initial meetings with parents, students, and tutors, and any necessary training. Obviously, the more people meeting with you in your office (home or otherwise), the more easily accessible and well decorated the office will need to be.

Beware!
The more strangers who come and go from your home, the more likely it is that something of value might go with them. Therefore, not unlike showing your home when selling it, you should make sure that valuable items are not in plain sight of visitors. While most people are inherently honest, there is no reason to tempt those who may not be.

Tutoring from Your Own Home

Less common, but still an option, is having students (or tutees) come to your home for tutoring. If you are a one-person operation, this means finding the quietest time in your household and/or having a separate room in which to provide tutoring. If you have tutors working for you, it means the same thing, times two if you want two tutoring sessions going on at once. It can get a little bit difficult juggling several tutoring sessions from your home, not to mention the parking situation and neighbors getting concerned about the volume of people coming and going from your home. You may also have certain tutors who want to tutor from their homes. Make sure they have the facilities to do so and live in a safe area. Then, make sure parents accompany their children and teens to the tutoring sessions.

Your Own Tutoring Facility

Neal Schwartz, whose Tutoring Club franchise is set up in a large, quiet office in Armonk, New York, uses dividers in one large room and has a second smaller room where a tutor and student can work. This allows for five or six tutoring sessions to take place at any given time at the one location.

The arguments for such a tutoring setup, or the "pros," are:

1. Students concentrate better when not at home with more potential distractions.

2. Tutors can go from one session to the next without having to incur travel time.

3. Any and all necessary materials, such as books, can be at the one location to assist tutors and students, if necessary.

4. The environment can be set up with proper lighting and furnishings conducive to learning and studying.

5. As an owner, you can monitor how things are going between tutors and students more closely and address concerns if they should arise.

6. You have a built-in location for tutor training.

7. You can accommodate two or three students in small study groups if you choose.

Of course, there's always the flip side. The negatives, or the "cons," are:

1. It can take time to find a suitable location.

2. The cost of renting, leasing, or buying such space can be high.

3. Setting up a space conducive to learning can also be costly.

4. More insurance is necessary to cover your location.

5. You'll need to find a location that has parking and is easily accessible to your core market.

The difference between one-to-one and classroom tutoring will be your choice. While one-to-one is typically considered more effective for tutoring, classroom work can also be helpful, provided you have small groups of students. In some instances, such as working toward essay exams or on broad concepts, students can benefit from ideas and conclusions presented by one another. Larger classroom settings can sometimes be helpful for test prep, but often hinder the actual tutoring of day-to-day class work since students are typically in different places, some falling far behind and others needing to understand formulas or specific lessons.

From a business standpoint, it's to your benefit to pay one tutor and have 20 students all learning at the same time. This is good for revenue, but typically doesn't work well in most tutoring situations and has gained a lot of criticism from those who don't see great benefits. In time, you can get a reputation for *not* meeting the needs of too many of your students because (as is often the case in the school setting) your review classes are catering to the middle of the group and not taking in the specific needs of various students. Again, your business should be predicated on the needs of the students. Tutoring is typically not designed to replicate the classroom, but to make up for that which students aren't getting from the school environment.

Online Tutoring

As online tutoring options continue to grow, so does the debate on the effectiveness of such tutoring. While online options open up a broader range of student–tutor possibilities, there are many old-schoolers who still have some concerns, such as Lynn Giese, president-elect of the National Tutoring Association. "I haven't had a lot of experience with online tutoring, but I'm still from the old school of one-to-one tutoring. You don't have the face-to-face when you're tutoring online. You want to see that they're getting it," says Giese, adding that technology continues to grow and with webcams and innovations, online tutoring may be more effective in the coming years.

Bright Idea
Take a look at tutoring from the client's perspective. While starting out in the tutoring business, consider what it is that your clients (the parents) are most concerned about when it comes to hiring a tutor. Here are five primary areas of focus for most parents.

1. **Credentials:** They want to see that the tutor has a certificate or has had training. Also, there is interest in how long the individual has been tutoring and his or her background in the specific area(s) of study.
2. **Location:** A tutoring facility? The student's home? The tutor's home? This is an important part of the equation for parents and one that varies depending on the age of the student and whether the parent can take time to travel to and from a tutoring location.
3. **A plan of action:** It's important that the tutor (and/or tutoring company) has a direction and a plan.
4. **Cost:** It's important to know the cost and how much time is included.
5. **Communications skills:** Parents want to see that the tutor has a sense of how to communicate effectively with their child—this includes everything from where the tutor sits to how he or she acts, body language, etc. Of course this will not be evident until after the first session or two.

Another concern raised by Mark Greenberg, founder of the International Tutoring Association, also an old-schooler when it comes to online tutoring, is that it can become like a homework helping service. "I saw one online advertisement asking kids to log in and get their homework done. The problem is that they don't really learn anything this way and while their homework is complete, they will bomb out on the next test," says Greenberg.

Despite some concerns, the online tutoring industry is growing quickly. Some institutions contract with an outside vendor to provide this service to students, while others create their own virtual tutoring programs. However, most schools cannot find the time or the manpower to institute their own online tutoring, so they opt to recommend outside services, which is where you come in. More about online tutoring in Chapter 9.

Finding a Location

Ultimately, the type of tutoring business you're considering will factor heavily into your choice of location. If you opt for a facility where students can come to meet tutors in either a one-on-one or classroom setting, you will need to find an easily accessible location with adequate parking for tutors, parents, and older students who drive. As is the case with most businesses, if you have clients coming to you, you will need to make them comfortable. Therefore, the location needs to be in a part of town that is easily accessible and makes parents, students, and tutors feel safe.

When you scout a location, you'll want to consider not only the cost to lease, rent, or even buy the facility, but other business location factors, such as:

1. **Your Neighbors:** What other types of businesses are surrounding yours?

2. **Noise Levels:** Is it a relatively quiet location?

3. **Proximity:** Are you within a reasonable travel distance from your major target market (20-minute drive or less)?

4. **Zoning:** What kind of zoning laws are in effect?

5. **Technical Needs:** Does the facility have the infrastructure to support your computer and other technical needs?

6. **Accessibility:** Are you near main roads and is there sufficient (free) parking?

7. **Economics:** Are there closed storefronts and boarded-up buildings, or does it look like a somewhat thriving area with new businesses?

8. **Safety:** Check with the local police precincts to find out if the area is considered "safe."

9. **Visibility:** You can always get more clients from passing foot and car traffic.

10. **Greenness:** Today, environmental concerns count in attracting clients and sav-

ing money. Is the location green? Can large windows minimize your heating bills? Is there some green area around the location? Can you make green accommodations and changes without much trouble? See if the location has some green potential.

Bright Idea

If you're going to run the business out of your home, check out the zoning laws carefully to find out what you can and can't do. Also, try to maintain a low profile so that you don't disrupt the neighborhood. Many neighbors have no problem with a small business being run from a home, provided you don't have a parade of people and delivery trucks showing up at all hours. If you foresee problems, get to know your neighborhood association and assure them that you won't be a nuisance.

Name That Business

A–Z Tutoring, Kaplan Learning Center, Tutoring 101, Strong Learning Centers, Three Rivers Tutoring, Bright Apple Tutoring, Eduwizards, and Tutorpedia are among the many names of tutoring businesses. While franchise businesses have already chosen a name for you, if you're starting your own tutoring enterprise, you're on your own. Unlike naming your son or daughter, who can have the same first name as millions of other Bobs, Jennifers, Staceys, or Phils, you'll be seeking a unique name that you can register your business under and use as your online domain name. Yes, today, finding a business name goes hand in hand with finding a domain name.

You want a name you can be proud of, one that identifies what you do and one that will be easy for clients to remember. If you can find a way to make yourself distinctive, that will be a plus. This can be in the form of your location, if you are the only tutoring business in a community, such as Myrtle Town Tutoring. It can also be combined with what you offer, such as Stamford SAT Prep Center, or what you hope to achieve, Straight "A" Tutoring. Of course, you cannot make any promises.

If you opt for "Learning Center" in your name, that can allow you more latitude to include tutoring and testing. Kaplan and Sylvan are two widely known learning centers that have locations all over the country. That doesn't mean you can't also be a learning center. You may decide to use your name to mark your territory within a larger area, such as Chelsea Learning Center, since Chelsea is a small, yet heavily populated section of Manhattan in New York City.

To find a name you like, you can start by making a list, then, not unlike Santa, checking it twice to see if you like the names before looking them up on the Internet and/or in the local business records to see if your name is already taken. Keep in mind

▲

that whatever name you go with, you and your staff will be repeating it every time you answer the phone. Sound out that name before you settle on it. Some names look great in print but are difficult, if not impossible, to understand over the phone. Other names are just long and cumbersome. Therefore, in a high-tech, web-savvy world, you want something that is easy to pronounce and easy to spell for your website.

Unless you're going online or planning to start a franchise, your local business can have the same name as a tutoring business thousands of miles away. However, you will want to register a domain name that is either the same as, or similar to, your business name, and you can't have the same domain name (web address) as someone else.

Bright Idea

If you're buying a domain name for your business, you want a .com name or possibly a .net name, only. The .org names are for nonprofits, .edu is for educational institutions, and .gov is for government agencies. Occasionally other suffixes pop up, but none have received much attention, so don't buy anything else, no matter who tells you that "It's going to be the next big thing."

Making Your Business Name Official

Once you've decided on a name, you'll need to register it. Make sure to do a business name search before registering. You do this for three reasons:

1. It ensures that nobody else in your area is using the name and gives you dibs on it.

2. It makes the IRS and your local authorities happy. Most cities or counties require that you have a fictitious business name or dba (doing business as). This way your business will go on public record, allowing those who want to look you up to do so.

3. Most banks won't allow you to open a business checking account—one with your company name, which gives you credibility—unless you can show them proof that you've registered a fictitious business name.

Obtaining a dba is quick and easy, and you can do it on your own. The process varies a bit in different states and counties, but the local licensing bureau will fill you in on what you need to do.

Domain Names

For your website, you will want to make sure the domain name is available and if so, register that name. Since so many domain names are already being used, you should think of several versions of the name in the event that one or more have already been taken.

One way to do a domain search is to type the name in your internet browser and see what comes up. You can also go to networksolutions.com and check to see if your name choices are available Following the easy directions, check to see if the domain name you've chosen has already been taken. If it has, choose another. When you find a permutation that's available, register it online. There are a number of companies through which you can buy and/or register domain names. You may also register some similar names if they are available, such as both the .com and .net suffixes of the name, or common misspellings. For example, if, while trying to go to Google.com, you type www.gogle.com, www.gooogle.com, or www.googel.com, you will still get www.google.com!

Determining Your Business Structure

For various reasons, including taxes and liability issues, it's important to think about how you want to structure your tutoring and/or test prep business. There are a few choices and you'll want to discuss them with your attorney and/or accountant before making a decision.

Sole Proprietorship: Sole proprietorship is, by all accounts, the easiest structure under which to run a business. You get a business license, file the applicable business forms for your state, and you're in business. It requires little paperwork and few formalities, other than paying taxes. Your income is reported on your personal or jointly filed tax return. The majority of small, individually run tutoring services are sole proprietorships. The drawback, however, is that if your business gets sued, so do you—personally. In other words, you are held liable, and it can put a serious dent in your personal finances. In a litigious society, you may want to take greater precautions. You can work closely with your attorney to come up with a contract that minimizes your responsibility regarding the results of your services. However, if you own a facility, you can still get sued if someone gets injured. If you're working from a home office, check your homeowners insurance to see what's covered. The problem is that there are, unfortunately, too many people today who come up with absurd reasons for lawsuits.

Incorporation: Should you choose to incorporate, you are essentially separating yourself personally from your business, which becomes a separate entity regarding liability and taxes. When you incorporate, the corporation carries the liability instead of you personally. You can also use such incorporation more effectively when negotiating with banks by reminding them the corporation guarantees the note. Even though the bank will probably still ask you for a personal guarantee, you can use your corporate status during such negotiations.

The biggest plus for incorporating, however, is that the business stands as a separate entity, meaning that you typically aren't personally held liable should there be a lawsuit. Instead, your company is sued and your personal assets are protected in most cases.

The negative aspect of incorporating is that you have a lot of paperwork and there are a number of rules you will need to follow, such as taking minutes at meetings and completing various forms. There is also the possibility of double taxation when you form a corporation, meaning you pay corporate taxes and then when you take money out of the corporation, you pay taxes again on your personal assets. You need to sit down with a business attorney or your accountant and weigh the plusses and minuses of incorporating, as well as how to avoid such double taxation.

LLC: A limited liability corporation (LLC) is another, newer option that's somewhat of a hybrid between incorporating and going solo. The advantages of forming an LLC are that you're afforded limited liability and have pass-through taxes similar to a partnership. By forming an LLC rather than a corporation, you receive nearly all the benefits of a corporation but avoid some of the drawbacks, such as double taxation, some requirements, and excessive paperwork. Again, you should discuss the pros and cons of your specific situation with your attorney and accountant.

Partnership: As for partnerships, proceed with caution. Make sure you have a partnership agreement spelled out detailing who is responsible for which tasks and functions. A partnership does not have to be a 50–50 split in regard to investing in the business, doing the work, or earning profits. You can have silent or active partners. You can have one or several partners. You can decide ahead of time who has more or less say in running the company, or you can have equal say. The most important thing is that you discuss and set up all this ahead of time. You'll need to have an attorney draw up such an agreement. There also need to be clear guidelines regarding how someone can leave the partnership or if the partnership is dissolved or sold. You may have a situation in which one partner takes full control and ownership of the tutoring business, while the other takes full control and ownership of the test prep business. You may also have a situation where one party wants to retire while the other wants to continue, but needs a new partner. There are many possibilities, so hash them all out with your attorney ahead of time. Also, go into partnerships with likeminded people and those whom you believe you can trust and rely on. Too many partnerships end good friendships or strain relationships.

From a business standpoint, partnerships are typically run in the same manner as a sole proprietorship, with each party claiming income on their individual tax returns. Of course, you can opt as partners to incorporate or form an LLC. Then you will need to discuss with an attorney how to structure the agreement favorably for all involved.

Contracts for Your Tutoring Business

Some tutoring businesses do not use contracts. Instead it's simply a pay-per-visit (hourly) rate and visits are scheduled on a one-by-one basis, or there is a regular agreed-on time each week. This can, and does, work for many tutoring businesses. However, should you start offering tutoring packages, or even in some cases, for a one-time tutoring session, you may want to have a contract in place outlining the responsibilities of both parties. Contracts provide parameters and offer you some form of signed paperwork in the event that any part of an agreement (typically verbal) is questioned. For example, if the parent claims that he or she heard a rate of $65 per hour, when the rate is $85 per hour, it's on paper.

Below is a basic sample contract that can be used between your tutoring service and clients. You can add other stipulations should you choose.

This contract made this _____ day of _____, 20___ is between _____ (Client/Student) and _____ (Parent or Legal Guardian) and Marvin's Tutoring.

Client has selected and agrees to hire Tutor for 6 one-hour sessions between _____ (Beginning Date) and _____ (Ending Date) at the rate of $____ per hour for tutoring in the following subjects:

_____

_____

The client agrees to pay the total of $____ on a _____ basis by check, cash, or money order made out to Marvin's Tutoring at the time of the scheduled session.

Client Cancellation:

Any changes in the scheduling need to be made prior to ___ hours of the scheduled session, or there will be a ___% charge added to the regular hourly fee.

Tutor Cancellation:

Should Tutor need to cancel a session, Client may reschedule for the same week or later in the calendar school year or ask for a different tutor by contacting Marvin's Tutoring. If a tutor cannot be found to fill in at the same time period, then the client will receive a ___% discount on the next tutoring session.

No-Show Policy:

Clients who are not present at the pre-determined location when Tutor arrives or who are more than ____ minutes late are considered no-shows. If Client is a no-show, he or she is still responsible for payment for the tutoring session.

Pay-per-session clients must present payment for the session in which he or she was a no-show and the following session in order for tutoring to continue.

Clients who arrive late will only be tutored for the remainder of the scheduled hour. There will be no prolonged sessions.

Schedule

Client and Tutor agree to the following tutoring schedule:

	Dates	Times
Session 1:		
Session 2:		
Session 3:		
Session 4:		
Session 5:		
Session 6:		

This contract is binding between all parties.

_____

Client/Student

_____

Parent or Legal Guardian of Client/Student

_____

Marvin's Tutoring

Contracting With Your Tutors

Of course, if you have pre-payment for x number of tutoring sessions, or have clients signing up for a class, you will need to stipulate what constitutes breaking the agreement. You should have a no-refund policy unless tutoring sessions or classes cannot be offered as agreed on in the contract.

The other contract you will want to draw up is that between yourself, on behalf of your business, and your tutors, who are, in essence, independent contractors. Such a contract needs to stipulate the responsibilities of the tutor and of your business in such an agreement.

Within such an agreement, you will want to outline a number of key points, including an agreed-on fee structure, which includes how much your business charges and how the tutor receives payment from your company (the tutor invoices you, you pay the tutor based on a time card, etc.). Other areas to be addressed in a contract with your tutors will be:

- **Scheduling:** The tutor is responsible for meeting the scheduling requirements that you have decided on. Therefore, if he or she has agreed to tutor 12 hours per week, then that is part of your signed agreement. If he or she cannot make a tutoring session, you will need to address how that will be handled.

- **Assigned Work:** The tutor will need to be responsible for having planned assignments for the student(s). Assignments can be created by the tutor, by your company with the tutor, or by your company, depending on how you choose to do business. In all cases, the agreement will need to state what the tutor will be responsible for.

- **Reviews:** Tutors need to be responsible for reviewing the work with students and apprising you of their progress. The manner in which you elect to handle this can vary (in-person meeting, e-mails, telephone discussion, etc.).

- **Conduct:** You should have a brief code of ethics and have your tutors sign it to confirm that they have read it. In the contract, you should also state that tutors are expected to conduct themselves in a professional manner at all times.

- **Termination:** Include grounds for termination.

- **Liability:** Cover yourself from tutor lawsuits by not allowing tutors to hold you responsible for personal injury or property damage resulting from their agreement to work with your business. Keep in mind that although this is part of the contract, you can still be sued if you are directly responsible for injury to a tutor.

- **Your Responsibilities:** The contract needs to point out how the tutor will benefit from this agreement. Your business will be responsible for marketing, scheduling, providing a tutoring location, etc. Whatever you're giving the tutor, put it in the contract. You will be responsible for living up to your end of the agreement, so only include what you know you can and will do for your tutors.

- **Taxes:** Make it clear that the tutor is not considered a full-time employee, but is an independent contractor, and spell out what taxes you and the tutor are and are not responsible for. Typically in such situations (depending on state law) you are not responsible for unemployment tax or workers' compensation, and the tutors are responsible for paying taxes based on their income. Review the tax situation with your accountant, based on state and federal laws at the time when the contract is drawn up.

The last part of an agreement is usually about the agreement being binding in your state and how disputes will be handled, which is typically by way of an outside party as decided by both parties. When your attorney reviews your contract, you can iron this out. You also want to include that the tutors may not solicit or take business away from your company without being held responsible in some manner.

Depending on the complexity of your business and your needs, your contract may have additional stipulations.

Attorneys and Accountants

Attorneys are like plumbers—you don't think about hiring one until you have an urgent problem. But as an entrepreneur, you should have a good attorney on retainer or at least available when necessary. You'll want someone who understands small business, and preferably someone well versed in the service industry. You will want your attorney to help you develop contracts with tutors and clients, as well as your lease and agreements with any vendors supplying you with books or other materials. Additionally, your attorney should review the privacy policy that goes on your website. When starting a business, you will need to have an attorney available fairly often. Once you are up and running, your legal needs should lessen.

Along with your attorney, you'll want to look into hiring an accountant who can help you make the most effective business decisions from a tax perspective. You'll be working with a lot of independent contractors, so you need to know what taxes you are and are not responsible for paying. You will also want an accountant to advise you of any special ways you can save money with your business structure, to oversee your operations, and to fill out those tax returns.

Know Your Insurance

Starting a business means you will be taking on new risks, some of which can be lessened by having the right insurance in place. You will want to consult with an insurance agent or broker to make sure you have the necessary coverage. If you know an insurance agent, or have a recommendation of someone who can offer you some good deals, then sit down and meet with this individual. If not, you might want to work with an insurance broker, who, unlike an agent, represents several insurance companies and may be able to find you a better rate. It's advisable to do some shopping and price comparisons before signing up for coverage. Insurancematch.com, Moneysupermarket.com, and a number of other Internet sites will come up if you do a search for "business insurance rates" or "business insurance comparisons."

What Do You Need

In an era when there are more than a dozen types of orange juice to choose from, it's not hard to imagine that there are numerous types of insurance offered. Basically you can get covered for anything, even a potential volcano eruption in New York City. The point is, you'll need to carefully consider the potential for various risks and buy the insurance you feel is most appropriate.

Most common types of insurance for a small business include:

- **General Liability:** For yourself and your tutors to be covered in your facility, or your home, this is essential. This will cover you if you're sued for damages resulting from an injury sustained on your property. This will also cover you against property damage that may occur on your property or (depending on the coverage) if you or one of your tutors breaks something on the property of a client. Review exactly what is and isn't covered and what you're not responsible for.

- **Equipment:** This is coverage of your equipment for damage or theft. If you are working at home, your home insurance may cover you. However, you may need a rider since you are now operating a business from your home. For a facility, this is especially important as it will protect any business equipment. Keep in mind that with laptops and cell phones, you may not need a lot of coverage, since much of your equipment (of any real value) will be portable.

- **Business Interruption Insurance:** If a fire, flood, theft, or natural disaster of any type shuts down your business, this insurance will cover you during the time you're getting your business up and running again. Don't underestimate the need for this insurance coverage.

If you have regular employees on your payroll, such as someone to answer the phones, you'll need to pay workers' compensation, which is now mandatory in all 50 states. This does not pertain to hiring tutors as independent contractors. You'll find other insurance, such as errors and omissions, and of course personal coverage for yourself, such as health insurance, which you may want to consider if you're not already covered.

When it comes to keeping your rates down, there are ways in which you can lower your insurance premiums. For example, if you have insurance to protect your equipment, your rates will be lowered if you have safety precautions such as locked drawers in which to keep smaller items and proper locks on doors and windows. The same holds true for your home insurance policies. The safer the home, the more likely you can keep your rates down, not unlike auto insurance, where better drivers without accidents or points on their licenses can get better rates.

Remember, when working with an insurance agent, make sure he or she is licensed in your state. You can also ask about getting specific riders to your homeowners policy if you're running your business from a home base. The National Consumer

Bright Idea

Sure, you can surf the web and get all sorts of names, numbers, and e-mail addresses for professionals, *but* it's advantageous to seek out attorneys, accountants, and insurance agents through recommendations from other business owners whom you trust. With this in mind, you may seek to join local organizations, associations, business groups, and/or the local chamber of commerce.

Insurance Helpline can be reached at (800) 942-4242, should you need assistance finding an insurance agent. You can also visit Local Insurance at www2.localinsurance.com.

Money: Finding It, Making It, and Spending It

Obviously, to make money in a business venture, you're going to have to start off with some money to spend. This can vary greatly depending on the type and size of your projected business. A homebased tutoring business can be launched for $1,000, while a franchise can cost $100,000 or more. So, where do you fall in that wide range of startup funding possibilities?

The size and scope of the business you hope to launch will depend largely on financing that you can:

- Take from your savings
- Accumulate by selling another business and/or personal assets
- Borrow from banks or lending institutions
- Borrow personally from friends, relatives, angel investors or elsewhere

Stat Fact
According to the National Tutoring Association, the number of individuals in the nation offering tutoring as a business has increased from 250,000 five years ago to more than 1 million today!

Startup Costs

Before you open any type of business, you will need to determine the various startup costs you could incur. This way, you will have an idea of how much money you will need.

For a homebased tutoring business, meaning you are working from your home, your expenses will include:

- Computer, printer, scanner, modem, and broadband Internet access
- Phones (including your cell phone and voice mail)
- Website design
- Business permits and licensing
- Office furniture
- Office supplies
- Market research
- Advertising and marketing to find tutors and students
- Attorney fees
- Accounting fees
- Insurance
- Printing costs
- Computer software
- Credit card processing capabilities
- Miscellaneous expenses

You can add to this list money for a training site if you don't think you'll be able to train tutors from your home or via the Internet. If you choose to open an office from which to run the business, but will still be sending tutors to students' homes, you can add in:

- Rent

- Utilities
- Cleaning and contracting or preparation

And if you'll have tutors and students working from a full-service location, you can add higher costs for rent, utilities, computers, office furniture, and supplies (all to accommodate the larger space), as well as more telephone expenses and higher insurance payments for more coverage. While it's possible that you may need some work done by a contractor in your home, it should be minimal for this type of business. However, if you set up shop in a larger location, you may need some work done to make the building meet your needs. Of course, this will be limited by what the landlord allows you to do. If you buy a building (which is not accounted for on the sample spreadsheet on the next page) you can do as you please.

⚠ Beware

A location can be ready to move into or need a significant amount of work to get it into shape for your specific business needs. Before committing to a "fixer upper," have a contractor and/or an engineer inspect the property to make sure you're not buying or leasing a place that requires far more work than you anticipate. You can find local engineers, building inspectors, and contractors in your local Yellow Pages or by doing a web search for your area.

Again, the $6,030 total on the sample spreadsheet can be reduced by $4,000 to $2,030 if you have all your computer/printer needs and set up your own website through Yahoo! or some other online means of building a simple site simply for promotional needs.

Also, don't forget that beyond startup costs, you need to have cash available to run the business from day one. Too many people neglect to add a cash reserve when

How Much Will It Cost to Start Up?

For a homebased business (assuming you have a computer already), you can start for under $2,500 (this means designing your own website or not having a site). For an office-based business, where you send tutors to students' homes, you are looking at roughly $10,000. An online tutoring business, because of the technical expertise required to get the system up and running (and maintain it) may cost roughly $25,000. A tutoring facility in which your tutors see students may cost upward of $50,000 if it's necessary to hire contractors; otherwise, you can probably get started for $25,000 with minimal contracting needs. Of course, if you're buying the land or the building, you can expect to spend much more. Tutoring franchises can range from $35,000 to over $250,000.

Sample Startup Costs

	Homebased	Outside Location (full tutoring facility)
Computers, Printers, Scanners	$1,000	$4,000
Internet Service (two months)	$40	$40
Phones and Voice Mail	$250	$500
Website Design	$3,000	$3,000*
Permits and Licensing	$200	$500
Office Furniture	$400	$2,000
Office Supplies	$50	$200
Market Research	$200	$200
Initial Advertising and Marketing	$300	$500
Attorney Fees	$200	$500
Accounting Fees	$100	$100
Insurance	$100	$500
Printing Costs	$70	$200
Computer Software	**	**
Credit Card Processing Capabilities	$50	$50
Miscellaneous	$70	$300
Rent (first two months)	N/A	$3,000
Cleaning and Contracting	N/A	$7,000***
Total Startup Costs	**$6,030**	**$23,090**

*This will cost more for actual online tutoring availability.
**Assuming you have basic software such as Microsoft Word and Excel.
*** Assuming you need only some minor work done on the facility.

determining their startup costs. Cash is important, so make sure you have reserve funds available.

Sample Startup Worksheet

	Homebased	Outside Location (full tutoring facility)
Computers, Printers, Scanners		
Internet Service (two months)		
Phones and Voice Mail		
Website Design		
Permits and Licensing		
Office Furniture		
Office Supplies		
Market Research		
Initial Advertising and Marketing		
Attorney Fees		
Accounting Fees		
Insurance		
Printing Costs		
Computer Software		
Credit Card Processing Capabilities		
Miscellaneous		
Rent (first two months)		
Cleaning and Contracting		
Total Startup Costs		

Financing

Now, looking at the costs, you can start to determine at what level you would like to approach this business. This will be based on the above-mentioned sources of financing, and how available they are for your needs. For example, how much of your savings can you devote to a business venture? How much do you feel confident that a commercial lender might give you? Let's evaluate the financing options more closely so you can determine which type of tutoring and/or test prep service might be realistic.

Savings: If you've earmarked money for opening a business and set it aside in a separate account, then you can look carefully at how much you have accrued and determine how much you can use to invest in yourself as an entrepreneur. Keep in mind that lenders like to see borrowers putting their own money into the business venture.

If you haven't been saving up for a business, you'll need to prioritize upcoming personal and family needs and then determine how much of your savings will be left over after college tuition, car and home loans, and other obligations and debts are covered. We don't suggest dipping into retirement savings, since you need to be prepared for your golden years, and it's getting harder to build up savings with a shaky economy. Nor do we suggest dipping into money saved up to meet your personal needs or those of your family.

Selling a Business or Personal Assets: If you already own a business, clearly selling it will bring you some capital. If you don't need the money for bailing yourself out of debt or for other immediate needs, this is a great way to finance your new venture. In some cases, you may be able to sell a portion of a business and start a second one. As for personal assets, you need to evaluate what you can and can't afford to part with comfortably. If you're empty nesters rattling around in a very large house, you might consider downsizing and using the extra money to start up a business, provided you have enough to cover your living expenses and retirement. Likewise, if you own a 1965 Mustang and would prefer to make a profit off your valuable possession and use that to fund your new business, that's another way to go.

Borrowing from Banks or Other Lending Institutions: The ease of obtaining loans from banks and credit unions will vary significantly depending on the going interest rate, the economic climate, your track record in business, and your credit rating. You'll want to get a hold of your credit report well in advance of launching your business. To do so, contact the three major credit bureaus, Experian (experian.com), Equifax (equifax.com), and Transunion (transunion.com). This way you can work on improving your credit rating if necessary by paying off outstanding debts and making sure they are reported to the credit bureaus. Also make sure there are no errors on your credit reports. While these three companies work diligently to maintain quality reports, there are numerous errors found. Contact the bureaus and make sure the errors are corrected if you find any.

Lending institutions want to know that you're a sound credit risk, and with that in mind, you'll be judged on your credit rating, your collateral, your business experience, and your own ability to invest in the business venture. They'll also want to know exactly what your plan is and why they should believe in your business (see Business Plans, below). Focus on these factors before going out to lenders. You can improve your credit rating, but it takes some time. Never trust anyone who advertises an overnight trick to turning around your credit score. They are almost always too good to be true and therefore are not legitimate. Collateral means putting up something to secure the loan. Avoid putting your home on the line.

Carefully consider assets you can use for collateral. As for your business experience, that should be clear in your business plan. If not, make sure you highlight exactly what you have done before that makes you the ideal person to open such a business. And finally, the more you're willing to put up of your own money (just as with a down payment on your home), the easier it is to get a loan. After all, lenders figure if you are willing to put your own money into this venture, you will take it more seriously than if you're simply relying on other people's money.

If you haven't run a business before, keep in mind that you can always start on a shoestring budget from savings or loans from friends and/or family and then run a business for a short time before working your way up to building a bigger business with bank or credit union financing.

> **Tip...**
>
> **Smart Tip**
> For information on starting and running a small business, as well as market research and guarantees on business loans, check out the SBA at sba.gov. Since 1953, the SBA has been helping entrepreneurs start, build, and run their small businesses.

Borrowing from Friends, Relatives, or Angels: Obviously the biggest concern when borrowing money from friends or family is straining the relationship. Therefore, you need to treat such a loan as you would treat a bank loan and write out some terms for paying back the loan. Hopefully it will be interest-free; if not, write out the terms of the interest. Seek out people who believe in your business goals and will be supportive. Also seek out people who won't expect that for their investment dollars, they'll have a controlling interest in how you run your business.

You may also seek out, and if you're lucky, find angel investors. These are individuals who back business ventures in hopes of making a profit down the road. In some cases they provide expert advice if they have been in the field, while in other cases they serve as silent backers. Typically, unless you are buying into a franchise, most tutoring businesses are not large enough to interest such angel investors.

There are people whom you will meet along the way, however, who might want to back you in a small way. Some young entrepreneurs gather a few thousand dollars through a variety of small loans from different sources. This can be an excellent way to gather some funding, provided you maintain control of your business and have a clear plan of how and when you'll pay back the loans with either interest or a predetermined percentage of the profits. Do your math carefully so you don't give everything away. If, for example, you determine that you need $15,000 to get the business off the ground and you put down $10,000 from your own savings and borrow $1,000 from each of five neighbors, with an agreement to pay them each $1,200 in two years (20 percent profit), then you essentially have an agreement from which you will spend $1,000 of your profits to pay off your $5,000 loan. A high rate of interest? Perhaps, but if you can't get a small term loan from a lending institution and this is a way to launch your business now, it's worthwhile.

You can also use a line of credit for short-term needs. A business line of credit is similar to your personal credit cards. You open a line of credit with a bank or credit union, and spend it as you need it.

Operating Costs

The other significant factor that you'll need to consider before moving full speed ahead is your operating costs. Starting a business is one thing. Running it on a daily, weekly, monthly, and annual basis is another. Remember, we've emphasized your need to have cash, or cash flow.

Typically operating costs are maintained on a monthly basis, since that's generally the time at which rent and utility bill payments are due. They differ from startup costs because these are the ongoing costs of running a business, as opposed to one-time permits or equipment purchases. Consider the following operating expenses:

- Rent (if you have an office or tutoring facility)
- Phone bills (including cell phone and voice mail)
- Other utilities (if you have an office or specific facility)
- Website costs
- Fees to tutors (and any office employees you hire to answer phones, etc.)
- Advertising and promotion (including printing)
- Postage and mailings
- Office supplies
- Insurance premiums
- Legal and accounting*
- Dues and subscriptions
- Miscellaneous

* Legal and accounting may not be monthly expenses, but may occur throughout the year, so you can take your estimated totals (e.g., $2,400 for legal and $1,800 for accounting) and divide by 12 for a monthly figure (e.g., $200 for legal and $150 for accounting).

Minimizing Operating Costs

Typically, it can routinely take a business two or three years to start showing a profit. As you build your business, it's always advantageous to consider ways you can minimize your operating costs wherever possible. Here are five cost-saving suggestions, some of which also double as eco-friendly business operating tips.

Since tutoring is typically an after-school activity, from 3:30 p.m. to 8:00 or 8:30 p.m., you might consider renting your space (if permitted by your landlord) to another business for the early part of the day. This needs to be a business that won't leave a mess for you to clean up. Another option is to share your space with another business until you are too large to do so any longer.

You can minimize your utility bills by using natural forms of heating and cooling, such as opening windows or wearing sweaters rather than running heat or air conditioning all the time. You might also consider passive solar heating and cooling, which means generating energy without the need to have mechanical systems installed. Keeping shades open and even installing a skylight can help warm a room through direct sunlight. Once this happens, if the room is sealed and the doors, windows, and skylights are kept closed, the hot air will remain inside during the evening hours. A floor that absorbs heat can also help. Conversely, shading and blocking sun on warm days, as well as keeping windows open in evening hours, can have the reverse effect, bringing in cooler air and keeping the temperature down by sealing in that air during the daytime. If this is done correctly, you can maximize your "natural" climate control and lower your utility bills significantly.

Another way to save on utility bills is to buy Energy Star–certified equipment (low energy) and use common-sense tips such as shutting down equipment when it's not being used or having computers go into sleep mode rather than using high-energy screen savers.

You can use word-of-mouth marketing to promote your tutoring business (which is the most-used method of promotion for most of the industry). If your tutors are helping students achieve better grades, the students will tell others, and you will get more business. Rather than expending money on advertising in magazines or on radio, you can start blogs and discussions online and find ways to get people talking about your business by giving them something unique to talk about (see Chapter 11 for more ideas).

Reuse office supplies and equipment and buy only what you need. Vast storerooms filled with 200 boxes of office supplies should be left for large corporations. Too many people buy far more than they need and do not reuse items. For example, you can save a lot of paper, not to mention trees, by printing on both sides of a piece of paper or not printing materials that you can e-mail to your tutors or students.

Minimizing paper needs and not wasting office supplies can be a cost saver that adds up, plus it can help you become a green business, which in today's eco-friendly culture is a good thing.

Paying Your Tutors

This is the toughest part of the business: How much do you pay your tutors, and how much do you get? Tutors can make anywhere from $25 to $150 an hour depending on their specialty, the geographic location, and the needs of the market. That means you'll have to determine a rate that's competitive in your area and provides your tutors with a living wage and your business with a profit. You'll pay tutors based on several factors including:

- Credentials (degrees and certificates)
- Tutoring experience
- Expertise in a certain area
- Comparable rates in your area

You need to establish rates and make sure that you're leaving yourself enough money to run the business and make a profit. Therefore, if some tutors are asking for too much money, you will have to find others. If, for example a tutor insists on $60 per hour, then you need to charge roughly $90 per hour to make money on the deal. This may or may not be too high a rate in a given area. Keep in mind that many tutors will say, "We don't need you, we can go it alone." While that's true, you can point out that you're paying to do the advertising and marketing, in many cases you're screening the clients, you're handling scheduling and in many cases you're screening the clients, handling scheduling, and possibly providing a location. This will make it more attractive for tutors to work with you than on their own ... plus you may have the necessary insurance coverage and, in some cases, even some benefits to offer by pooling tutors as a group.

Making a Profit

This is where you'll need to start crunching numbers with your accountant. You'll need to determine how many tutor-hours you'll need per month to maintain your business. This will depend largely on your initial market research. How many students need tutoring? How much competition is there in your area? How much can you take as your slice of the overall pie?

Let's try to figure out a hypothetical situation for a tutoring business.

Two neighborhoods within a five-mile radius have five schools from K through 12th grade totaling 2,000 students. You estimate, based on your research regarding the number of students using tutors or test prep (and the state of the economy), that

10 percent of these students will use tutors. Therefore, the population of students in this area that's estimated to be using tutors is 200.

Now assume that there are two other tutoring businesses in the immediate vicinity, so you'll be slicing the market three ways. Add to that independent tutors and online tutors as one category and you'll be slicing the pie four ways, one for each of the other two businesses, one for the online and independent tutors together, and one for yourself. Therefore, you could draw 25 percent of the 200 potential students, or a total of 50 students. Of course, being new, let's say you attract only 35 students. If these students came an average of twice a week, you would have 70 student tutoring hours a week or, if you are open on Saturday, 13 per day.

If you charge $70 an hour, paying the tutors 50 percent or $35 per hour, you would make $2,450 per week, or roughly $10,000 per month on average (70 hours × $35 = $2,450 per week). That would come to $127,400 annually.

If you have calculated your monthly expenses at $5,000 per month, beyond paying the tutors (since we've already deducted that amount), you will make the remaining $5,000 per month, or $60,000 income, some of which will go back into the business in the early years to keep it growing. Of course, for many businesses in the early going such profits simply are not possible, considering startup costs also need to be deducted and it's often hard to build up a steady flow of customers right off the bat—this is why most businesses take anywhere from two to five years to see a profit, depending on the size of the business, the amount of marketing, and the expenses to run it.

If you're working from home, you can bring that number up through a lower overhead. Of course it will take some time to build up to 35 regular clients and you'll need several tutors to handle that amount, as well as a few on call should your regular tutors phone in sick or be unable to make sessions. If your tutors are asking for more money, then either you will keep a little bit less, or charge a little bit more, depending on what is an affordable rate in your market. Know the going rate that tutors are taking home in your area, since you'll need to match it to be competitive. Tutors who can make $60 an hour will not want to work for you for $40 an hour, unless they can't get enough volume at their rate or they're wasting additional hours on scheduling and spending money on marketing themselves.

The example above is rather simple. It will take some due diligence to determine the size of your target market and how much you can charge. The point is, however, that once you look at the potential number of students and tutoring hours and determine a price that fits the economics of the community, you can begin to figure out your possible income after expenses.

The Business Plan

You've probably heard it mentioned many times, but the truth is, a business plan is an important document for all new (and current) businesses. Whether you're opening a small part-time tutoring service or launching a major operation, a business plan is worthwhile for several reasons, including:

- Helping you procure funding

- Helping you attract quality personnel (in this case, good tutors)

- Providing a guideline to get your business on track and steer it toward the future

These are all reasons why business owners should take some time to put such a plan together. In fact, the process of writing a business plan can, and typically will, help you think through all the various aspects of your pending business. It provides you with a "blueprint" so that no stone is left unturned. It's a living document that serves as a benchmark and can be altered and expanded as your business grows and changes over the years.

There are many business plan websites and software templates that can guide you through the process. They differ slightly, but most include the following sections:

- **Executive Summary:** This is a short, broad, yet enticing summary of the business. What is the business all about and why are you excited about it? Although it usually appears first, this part is typically written last, after you have put all the pieces in place.

- **Services and Products:** Here you can include specific subjects your tutors will teach and all of the services offered (test prep, homework help, etc.). If you sell any products, such as books, notebooks, or snacks, add that in here, as well. Also include services or products you anticipate selling later on.

- **Industry Analysis:** Here you will paint a picture of the overall tutoring industry and where you will fit into this market. From your research, talk about the "big picture." By researching and writing about the tutoring business, you'll learn more about the industry in which you are about to embark.

- **Competitive Analysis:** This is a biggie. Do your research carefully and know whom you are up against. Be realistic and list the strengths and weaknesses of the most direct competitors. Don't forget to mention online tutoring, which is less direct, but still competition. Then, see if you can provide a service that others are not providing. Review what other businesses are doing by answering the question, "Why would someone come to you over the other tutoring businesses in the area?" This can be your competitive edge.

- **Marketing and Sales:** Now that you have plenty of details regarding the services you will be providing, you need to explain how you'll let the world know that you're in business. In this section, discuss your plans for marketing and promoting your tutoring business. Are you marketing your services on the Internet? If so, how will people find your website? Where do you plan to advertise and why did you select such options? Are you printing and mailing out flyers? This is where to define your plan of attack. If you're seeking funding, this is an important section.

Some people like to have a full-fledged marketing plan. As a small service-oriented business, you may or may not want to put together such a detailed plan. You will, however, need to think through and write about some of the places in which you plan to advertise and market the business, as well as the costs for doing so. Remember, many tutoring businesses survive largely on word-of-mouth marketing and a little bit of advertising and promotion.

- **Management:** Another key section is management, where you'll list who will run the business. Potential financial backers will be particularly interested in this information, since they want to know to whom they are lending their money. Include all the key people involved in making this business happen. If this is a solo venture, use a biography that features experiences in your career or personal life that apply to this venture. If you have web designers or technical help, as well as anyone putting together specific educational programs for your tutoring business, include them briefly as well.

- **Operations:** From your daily hours of operations to the logistics of the business (tutors going to students' homes, students coming to your facility, etc.) this will need to be outlined. If you're doing one-on-one tutoring and classes, explain when, where, and why you're using both modes of education. If you'll be doing seminars or webinars or keeping an inventory of books, explain. Walk the reader through a virtual tour of what would be going on if they were to visit the facility or your office. For homebased business owners, you can simply describe your home office.

- **Financial Pages or Forms:** The goal here is, with a little help from your accountant or financial planner, to make realistic projections based on researching similar businesses. Here is where you show the math we demonstrated earlier and then project profits and losses over a year. Because of startup costs, it may take a year or two to show a profit if you're starting a large tutoring business or buying a franchise. You'll need to cover startup expenses. If you're homebased, you may be able to forecast profits in a matter of months. The more money involved, the more detailed you'll make this section. After all, if you're buying a business or a franchise and are borrowing money, lenders will want to see when they can expect to get their money back. Hint: Be conservative in your financial estimates.

- **Financial Requirements:** This is very important, if you're seeking funding. This is where you include the amount of financing needed, based on the previous sections, to reach your goals. Again, be realistic, research costs carefully, and indicate how much money you anticipate putting into the business venture yourself. As mentioned earlier, you stand a greater chance of getting investors interested, or bankers to approve a loan, if you've invested some of your own money into the business.

Add to this supporting documentation, which will include various financial reports, and you'll have a business plan. Don't try to dazzle prospective readers with hype, but provide the real story of the business so that it's clear on paper how it will operate and when you anticipate making money.

This is a very basic outline. Before you sit down and start writing, you'll need to do research and look at other business plans in books or online to see the phrasing and style of such a business plan. Investors can see through exaggerations … plus you don't want to fool yourself into thinking you'll be making more money than is practical for a new business.

You should put on a cover page and try to have a neat and error-free document if you'll be showing it to other people. If it's for yourself, you need not worry as much, but you should have the plan well organized and easy to read so you can use it as a guide.

The most important thing about a business plan is that it should read like a well-organized document that tells the story of your upcoming business. If you're looking to use it to obtain funds, make sure you can answer all possible questions that might be raised by your business plan. If you're asked to explain something and can't, you can kiss that source of funding goodbye. Therefore, be ready to back up your plan wholeheartedly.

As your business grows and changes, you'll want to review the plan and even update it.

Business Plan Books

Business Plans Made Easy by David H. Bangs Jr., Entrepreneur Press

Your First Business Plan: A Simple Question and Answer Format Designed to Help You Write Your Own Plan by Brian Hazelgren, Sourcebooks, Inc.

How to Write a Business Plan by Mike P. McKeever, NOLO Press

How Tutors
Help Students

As is the case with any business, the more you know, the better equipped you are to handle all situations that arise … not to mention sounding intelligent when discussing your industry. While you may not be doing any tutoring yourself, you should be knowledgeable about the various types of learning and training that tutors can provide.

Types of Learning

In this chapter, we first look at some of the various types of learning.

The Visual Learner: Visual learners will be the first to agree that a picture is worth a thousand words … or more. They tend to learn most effectively from visual images, including photos, visual displays, videos, and even diagrams. In classroom settings, and even while working one-on-one with a tutor, the visual learner can benefit from a variety of visual stimuli, including facial expressions and gestures. Using drawings, flash cards, color-coded materials, print-outs, maps, highlighters, charts, photos, visual analogies, and diagrams to enhance a lesson will be of great benefit to this type of learner. Watching a play, for example, such as the musical *1776*, can be a wonderful way to teach history to a visual learner.

The Auditory Learner: Lectures, discussions, talking, singing, and sounds are significant to the learning process for someone who learns via their auditory senses. Books on tape can be a big plus for someone who takes in information effectively in this manner. You can spot auditory learners because they very often remember exactly what they've heard and respond well to audio tapes and group discussions. For a tutor, reading passages aloud, talking about the material, replaying tapes of lectures, emphasizing key points with a change in inflection or tone of voice, and asking students to paraphrase material aloud can make a difference for this type of learner.

The Tactile or Kinesthetic Learner: These are individuals who learn most effectively from a hands-on approach, which includes touching and exploring. A tactile/kinesthetic learner wants to "do things," get involved in the process physically, and can benefit from class field trips and by experiencing the process of learning through taking part in the activity. Working with this type of learner means letting them get involved in a physical process or a task that makes the learning experience come to life for them. Note taking, underlining key words, or highlighting passages can be helpful for such a student. Also, working in a lab environment, taking a field trip, playing a game, or doing an actual demonstration are part of the process, as they allow this type of learner to be involved. Acting out a scene in history can be a great way for this student to learn.

These are the three ways in which learning styles are divided into groups based on sensory input. From working with a student, tutors can determine which of these ways can be most effective.

Another manner in which learning is approached is through the active and passive (or reflective) means. Active learning involves students working on activities, much like tactile/kinesthetic learning. Whether individually or in groups, working on projects or problem solving, active learning means doing as opposed to listening and taking in a lecture. For children (or adults) who find it hard to sit still and listen, this is a more hands-on approach to learning.

The opposite of active learning is passive or reflective learning. Reflective learners focus on taking in information and then thinking about it, or reflecting on it. The process may include digesting the information, reviewing and/or summarizing it, and later formulating theories, ideas, or questions based on what was absorbed from the materials. Another manner of reflective learning can be theorizing, in which the individual forms a theory based on their understanding and analysis of material presented.

Again, determining whether a student is more likely to benefit from active or passive learning should be part of the tutor's assessment.

Another type of learning distinction popularized from research beginning in the mid-1970s and continued through the early 1990s focuses on what is called deep versus surface learning. While one would immediately assume that it is more important to have a "deeper" understanding of a subject, that's not necessarily the case. Tutors and students need to make a judgment call regarding which is best in a given situation.

Deep learning includes a focus on the underlying roots and the meaning behind the material presented. It may include knowledge from other sources, other classes, or daily life. Such learning is based on a greater conceptual knowledge from within the student, hence the term "deep." Surface learning focuses on the immediate task at hand. It centers on the information itself and there is no other internal or outside information involved, although students may have tricks or processes for memorizing such material. The emphasis here is based on fulfilling that which needs to be learned for the test or overall grade or assessment.

While deep learning is more likely to be retained for a longer time, and more valuable in the future, there are circumstances where surface learning is necessary, such as a short window in which to learn material that is primarily memorization. In a culture where mandatory testing has taken precedence in the schools, many teachers and students are forced into surface learning to meet academic requirements. Tutors and students need to determine which meets the immediate needs of the student.

A Flexible Approach

Sylvan Learning Centers, which are among the most successful learning centers in the country, take pride in using a flexible approach to learning and focusing on the needs of the individual students. One-size-fits-all rarely works when it comes to teaching effectively. There is no single "correct" way to learn and no learning style is the "best" method across the board. Learning is also not really about intelligence. Yes, some people have the capacity to learn more easily and retain more information than others. However, in the right setting, with the right learning approach, people can reach significant levels of knowledge. In fact, most people, due to a number of external factors (such as poor nutrition, poor study habits, being in distracting environments, learning disabilities, etc.) do not come close to their potential. To teach effectively, it's necessary to gauge the way the learner, or student, best takes in material, since we all learn differently. Good teachers know how to reach different types of learners in the same classroom, either through breaking up the materials or varying the way in which they teach a lesson (some auditory components, some visual, some hands-on). They can reach more students than those who stick with only one method and aren't in touch with the learning styles of their students. Of course, it can be difficult for a teacher in a room full of 25 diverse students to reach everyone. However, in one-on-one tutoring or even in small groups (divided into similar types of learners), it should be much easier to reach more students through effective tutoring ... which means teaching toward the learning style of each student.

Stat Fact

It is estimated, as of 2008, that nearly 10 percent of school-age children and teens in the United States have a learning disability, falling into one of a number of categories including dyslexia and ADD or ADHD.

Working With Learning-Disabled Students

Learning disability (LD) is a broad term, one with numerous subcategories. For that reason, there's no single definition to define all learning disabilities, since difficulties can be linked to reading, math, comprehension skills, language-based skills, writing skills, and/or reasoning skills. In some cases problems will range across several of these areas, while in other cases they will be focused in one area.

Typically LD students are unable to keep up with the academics as they are being taught in the schools. These students are generally two years behind in their scores on tests and their reading and/or math levels. Of course, students may fall behind in school for numerous reasons.

While some learning disabilities are the result of environmental factors, and some are behavioral issues as opposed to actual learning disabilities, we should also note that very often LD is hereditary and that such disabilities should not be confused with physical or other disabilities, such as autism or behavioral disorders.

Parents should be involved in the process of having their children tested and learn about their child's learning disabilities from the school's assessment. Hopefully they will see progress from the interventions taken in the school. From that point, the tutor can pick up on what is being done to help the student in the school, as long as progress is being made. After all, it doesn't help to continue with methods that aren't working. For some students, it's a comprehension issue that needs to be addressed, while for others it is a language-based problem.

Unfortunately, many LD students are either not tested or the root of the problem isn't discovered by standardized testing. The problem is that the typical means of testing is standardized across the board and applies to learning based on traditional methods within the school. The testing typically used, known as the Discrepancy Model, does not account for many factors outside the typical realm of learning and comprehension. For example, many children have poor nutrition that can affect their performance in schools while others suffer from allergies, and some have emotional problems (which may be related to their home environment). Other students have visual or auditory problems that can be corrected (in most cases) by visiting the appropriate doctor.

There are also those who have processing issues. For example, one such processing issue, called Irlen Syndrome, named for its discoverer, affects several million students and typically falls between the cracks, not being picked up by standardized testing. Irlen Syndrome is a processing issue between the eyes and the brain. It's not a visual problem, so it isn't detected by an optometrist, and it's not a comprehension or learning issue, so it's not detected by the teachers or guidance counselors administering the tests. A child with Irlen Syndrome looks at words, letters, or numbers on a page (or a white board, computer screen, etc.), but he or she does not see steady, clear words and letters. Just as when you look at an optical illusion that appears to be moving on the page, the brains of these children don't process the words, letters, or numbers in a stationary or comfortable manner. In some cases they all bunch together, while for others they look like they are dancing.

The idea that everyone looks at a sheet of paper and sees it the same way is wrong, and that's because everyone's brain works differently. In this case, the manner in which light is being filtered into the eyes affects the way the person processes the information. For people with Irlen Syndrome, there are Irlen Centers set up around the country and around the world that fit individuals for the appropriate colored filters that make what's on the page, white board, etc., appear still. This is just one of many possible problem areas that are not clearly defined. Therefore, it can be difficult as a tutor of children with learning disabilities to develop an effective learning plan for each student.

As a tutor, you're not in a position to diagnose anyone or anything—that's not your job. However, if you detect that standard methods of learning are not helping, and have the sense that the student may need to be tested for visual, hearing, or processing problems, you should discuss the matter with the parents of the student, or the student themselves if they are over 18.

Working with learning-disabled students can be challenging. You want to find specially trained tutors to handle these situations. Those tutors who are able to make great progress with LD students find it very rewarding.

From your perspective as a business owner, you will want to find people trained to work with students having ADD/ADHD, dyslexia, and other commonly diagnosed learning disabilities.

The Ways and Means of Tutoring

Most tutors will agree that when working one-on-one with students you should have various options at your disposal, since the students will present different needs and challenges. Some students need you to walk them through material, while others can handle more on their own and require your help simply to stay on track. The best tutors adjust to the style that best helps each specific student. Among the options, when it comes to a tutor/student interaction, are the following:

Explaining Material: When necessary, a student may simply be lost. New material that a student may have missed, or a subject in which the student has clearly fallen far behind, may require the tutor to play the role of teacher for a while and explain the material in a manner that suits the grade level of the student and the type of learner, as noted above. While tutors don't want to be "teaching" (as opposed to tutoring) in most cases, there will be times when such explanations are required to get the student caught up or back on track. Therefore, a good tutor needs to have a knack for explaining things clearly … and making sure the student "gets it."

Guiding or Supporting a Student Through Homework or Study Materials: One of the most common ways of tutoring is reviewing and helping a student with work in a specific subject. This is typically presented in the form of homework or study materials for an upcoming exam. Such situations don't mean that the tutor should be doing the homework assignment, but instead, like a driving instructor, trying to keep the student on the road with guidance, suggestions, and reassurance. The goal of the tutor is to let the student lead the way if possible. If not, he or she can move the process along by keeping the student on track as they move from one problem or reading passage to the next.

Asking Key Questions: One way to make students think and express their knowledge in a specific area is by asking questions to see if they understand the work. For more broad-based subjects, such as studying for an essay test or an exam on a book that they have just read, the tutor will want to ask broader questions that let the students expound on what they know. Obviously, for cut-and-dried, fact-based answers, such as dates or other memorized materials, the tutor will want to ask more specific questions. Since test questions are not always straightforward, it helps if a tutor asks questions in a variety of ways to see if the student can approach the material from different vantage points.

Finding New Ways to Present Materials: For younger students in particular, this

The Tutor Stays in Control

Tutors always need to remember that they are in control. Manipulative students who get the tutor to help them hand in exemplary work while still not fully understanding the material are not helping themselves. After all, the tutor can't take the test for a student. Tutors must always stop and assess who is in control if it appears that a student or the student's parents are manipulating the situation. While a tutor can do what is asked by a parent (who is footing the bill), the tutor should make it clear when he or she believes that the request is not really helping the student.

is especially important. Some kids aren't fond of school, so if your methods do nothing more than mimic the school experience, you may be shutting down the lines of communications. Finding new ways to present the material, which can mean through charts, graphs, songs, drawings, or even a puppet show, can add to your teaching repertoire. Remember to keep in mind the manner in which your student seems to learn best (visual, auditory, tactile, etc.).

In addition to these and other means of tutoring, there are other factors that tutors should keep in mind while working with students on an individual basis. For example, silence is okay. The tutor need not fill in every moment. Letting a child silently work on a problem or ponder an answer for a few seconds is all right. Tutors need to be patient and not jump the gun. It's important that the student is pushed to use his or her brain and does the work.

On doing good work and getting the answers right, it's always beneficial for a tutor to be reassuring. Students like to know when they are doing well and a little reassurance goes a long way.

Know Your Students

The best tutors have developed their own ways and means of assessing their students' abilities, and they essentially "know their students." They have a good idea of where their students are in their schoolwork, how they best learn, and what shortcomings or difficulties they have when trying to complete their work.

Not unlike a therapist or a doctor, there is nothing wrong with a tutor jotting down some notes after they've worked with a student. These can be shared with you as the owner of the business, or not, depending on how you've set up the business model. Are you involved in the tutoring process, overseeing how students are doing, or is the progress solely up to the tutor? Your background as an educator or a businessperson will likely factor into how well you know the progress of each student. You should always be apprised at least in a general manner as to the overall progress of the students being helped by your tutors, since it is you who will get the phone calls from parents when things are not going well. Conversely, you want to know that your business is serving the intended purpose—helping students learn and improve their grades and test performance.

Tutors who know their students well are usually retained the longest and requested when the student's brother or sister needs help a year or two later. It's therefore beneficial to you as a business owner to impress on all of your tutors that they take the time to get to know and understand their students in a professional manner. It's also important to make time to meet with your tutors and get regular updates on their students. Together, you and your tutors should have an idea of the progress students are making.

Tutoring Groups or Classes

Tutors in group situations often operate more closely to a teaching modality than to a tutoring situation. The difference, however, is that students are coming to such a class, session, or workshop to get help rather than worry about your assessment of their work. After all, you're not grading them in any formal manner. Instead, they can focus on reviewing information and learn to fill in the gaps. Less pressure should allow for easier communication between the tutor and student. While some businesses will pack more students into a class to bring in more money, it's beneficial to the students to keep such classroom-style tutoring session relatively small, at less than 10 students: typically three to five works best.

As mentioned earlier, the benefit of group or class tutoring is that students can help one another by presenting different viewpoints, asking questions that other students may not have thought of, and even answering each other's questions. A tutor needs to be prepared to explain some information, while opening up the floor for questions and discussions on other material. It's important that the tutor tries to make all students feel comfortable and encourages all to participate without any students dominating or any students left out.

Tutors should be able to gauge individual students as they do individualized work within a group session. They can also get a feel from the group as a whole as to the pace at which it can work.

One of the most important factors in facilitating a productive group setting is for the tutor to set up some general guidelines in the beginning and maintain control. As the owner of the tutoring facility, you can put in writing some general guidelines, such as:

- Do not interrupt other students.
- Criticize ideas and not other people.
- Be respectful of the tutor.

- Don't eat during the session.

Include whatever you like, while keeping it brief. The point is that you can provide a general structure and the tutors can provide their own guidelines and structure.

When hiring tutors, which will be discussed later in the book, you should ask about their means of assessing students and how they determine the best manner of teaching a given student or structuring a group. Be in a position to discuss such methods of learning with your tutors. If you have specific methods you believe are effective, you can train your tutors in that methodology. However, taking into account the differences in tutors and in students and having some flexibility is very much recommended.

Stat Fact

To give you an idea of how important tutoring is today, it's estimated that nearly 70 percent of middle and high school students in the United States read below grade level. In addition, of 156 United Nations member countries listed, the United States ranks 49th in literacy.

7

Finding and Keeping Tutors

As is the case in any business, you want to have good, reliable, qualified individuals working for your business. These are the people who will represent your company in the tutoring world, and, quite frankly, they can make or break you. They can be your best sales reps. "You want to work with tutors who are going to recommend your business and represent your name out there in a positive manner," says Laurie Hurley, owner of Home Tutoring Business and creator of Accounting Tools for Tutors. Unprofessional behavior by tutors can be your downfall, since word of mouth can be as damaging as it can be beneficial to the future of your business.

Why Should Tutors Work for You?

If a tutor puts up a few signs around town in store windows or on bulletin boards letting it be known that he or she is tutoring in a particular subject (or several subjects), he or she can find clients and be a one-person operation. So why should a tutor work with you? Here are a few reasons:

Tutoring Experience: Many college students and younger teachers have not tutored before and it's a way of getting trained (by you or your staff) and getting started.

Larger Market: Many potential customers see the signs posted on bulletin boards in local stores, or in penny savers, but only a small percentage call. An even smaller percentage actually book sessions. You, however, can afford to market and promote on a wider level.

Credibility: Unless an independent tutor comes well-recommended, he or she is not likely part of any larger organization. Being attached to a tutoring business or learning center can enhance the tutor's credibility.

Convenience: If you have a location at which tutoring takes place, the tutor can see four or five students in one place and not have to drive from house to house or have a parade of people in and out of their home.

Insurance: If someone gets injured at your location, it's better for the tutor than if someone gets injured at the tutor's home. If there's any type of legal dispute regarding the actions of a tutor, he or she has the backing of a business.

Scheduling Headaches, Paperwork, and Phone Calls: You handle all this, which can be especially helpful for a tutor who's likely busy at another job during the day.

In short, there are a number of good reasons for tutors to work through a business. While they can charge more on their own, it's harder to find and screen students and easier to run into more difficulty without the backing of a company behind them.

But Can They Teach?

Teachers, former teachers, assistant teachers, college students, and experts in the fields of mathematics, writing, history, and other areas may all qualify to be tutors. You need to spread the word that you are looking, hiring, and paying tutors. A Tutors Wanted ad in the local papers is one simple way to bring in qualified candidates. Also,

Tip...

Smart Tip

Before advertising for tutors, take a look in local publications or online, and see if you can find some other ads for tutors. This will give you an idea of what to put in your ad copy. Below is a sample tutor ad from a website.

Tutors Wanted

Flexible weekly schedule

Competitive pay

REQUIREMENTS: The ideal tutor is a college graduate with 2 years of previous teaching/tutoring experience, a minimum 3.0 GPA, excellent SAT (1300) or ACT scores (28 composite), and reliable access to a car.

You can be more or less specific in your requirements and also include geographic areas in which you need tutors.

posting signs at colleges and ads in college papers can generate responses, as well as visiting schools and getting to know some staff personnel. You'll also find discussion boards and other online places where teachers communicate. Typically, once you get a few interested parties, you'll build your base of tutors through word of mouth, much as you build your customer base. Teachers and students know other teachers and students who may also be interested in tutoring.

Another Sample Ad for Tutors

Ad Copy: Looking for tutors for middle and high school students in academic subjects that match your expertise and experience (math, science, English, writing, and foreign languages). Along with tutoring students in their ongoing class work, you will tutor students who are preparing to take the SAT, ACT, or SAT II subject tests. This is a fantastic opportunity for you to share your knowledge with students, and serve as both a role model and mentor.

We offer a flexible 5- to 20-hour schedule, including afternoons, weeknights, and/or Saturday afternoons. Starting pay is $25–35 per hour depending on experience. We provide training and give bonuses.

What to Look For in a Tutor

We started to discuss qualities to look for in a tutor way back in Chapter 2.

Now, let's take a closer look at what the best tutors have in common. Besides having credentials, expertise in their fields, clean backgrounds, flexible schedules, and good communication skills, good tutors know how to connect with each of their students. They can clearly discern whether a student is "getting it" or not. They can seek ways to bring material to life for the student who is lost, even if he or she is saying, "Sure, I understand." As is the case with a good salesperson, a good tutor can read people's body language, hear what they are saying, and see when there's a communication breakdown.

Experience is important, even more so than a degree in education. Being able to teach doesn't mean you can tutor. There are subtle but real differences, and good teachers don't necessarily translate automatically into good tutors. Tutors who have experience will be better prepared to deal with the different situations that arise and the variety of students, parents, and personalities. They will often have experienced similar situations or personalities in the past and will be better equipped to handle them.

Interviewing Potential Tutors

There are several things you'll want to find out during the interview process. Obviously, experience, credentials, availability, and pay rate will be discussed, or appear on the applicant's resume and/or your application form. Having each person fill out an application ahead of time can cut down on some of the interviewing and note taking during an interview, leaving you open to focus on more significant concerns. Make the application simple to fill out, including only necessary information for your purposes.

Areas you will want to cover in an interview include:

- The individual's tutoring style
- How the tutor prepares for a tutoring session
- How the tutor starts a session
- How he or she keeps parents abreast of the student's progress
- How he or she charts or monitors the student's progress from session to session
- What tools the tutor uses, such as books and/or lesson plans
- How he or she handles some common situations, such as the lazy student, the student who is trying to get the tutor to give them the answers or do their homework for them, the student with obvious learning or behavioral issues, etc.

You then need to determine the tutor's availability and make it clear that you need dependability. Therefore, even if someone can only tutor five hours a week, you need to make sure that tutor can commit to those hours. Tutoring business owners agree that the worst scenario is having unreliable tutors and that you cannot keep such people in your organization.

As is the case with any job interview, you want to assess the positive qualities of the candidates and determine how they will excel in the actual work situation, which in this case is working with students and communicating with parents.

In the case of peer tutoring, you'll want to interview and then train students to help other students. "It works as long as your tutors are trained and meet tutoring standards," says Lynn Giese, who heads the program for Columbus State Community College and is a board member of the National Tutoring Association (NTA). "I use the NTA standards so that tutors know what's expected of them and how to perform in a tutoring setting. Obviously, the tutor also needs to have a good understanding of the subject that they're tutoring," adds Giese.

In answer to the question "Who makes a good tutor?" Giese adds, "The student has to have a recommendation from their instructor and they have to have an A or a B in the class to be considered as a possible tutor. Then they go through the hiring process here at the college. Once I interview them we do background checks and all of that." explains Giese.

Background checks and talking to references are important before hiring any tutors. Don't take shortcuts. One bad apple can spoil your entire business.

Feedback from Students

"So, how am I doing?" former New York City mayor Ed Koch used to ask all the time while in office. You need to ask how your tutors are doing and get feedback from student and parents. You can call the parent(s) after one session to make sure everything went smoothly and then perhaps send a form after a couple of months to check in on how the tutor is doing with the student. Assessments of tutors are very important. On a short questionnaire to parents, you might ask:

- Is he or she punctual for tutoring sessions?
- Is he or she professional during tutoring sessions?
- Does he or she come to sessions prepared?
- Is he or she responsive to the needs of your son or daughter?
- Does he or she provide feedback on how your son or daughter is doing?
- Do you see any improvement in your child's work in the area of tutoring?

▲

You've Got Personality

Do your tutors have the right personality? Proficiency in a subject area is not enough. While you need not find entertainers, you want tutors who have a way of making subjects come to life, and as a result, keeping students engaged in the material. In an age of iPods, IMs, and constant stimulation, you need tutors who can get through to students and hold their interest despite the ever-shortening attention span of the Facebook/IM generation. Some tutors look for signs of students' interests or hobbies to use as common denominators, such as the student who comes in wearing a baseball cap of his or her favorite team. Peer tutors can discuss common interests at the school they both attend.

Along with finding some common ground, tutors need to add a little "pizzazz" to what can be tedious work for the student. Look for tutors who have a little something extra when it comes to personality, as it can go a long way toward successful tutoring.

Can You Keep Them Coming Back?
(Availability and Reliability)

"One of the toughest things is finding people who will stick around a while," says Neal Schwartz of the Tutoring Club in Armonk, New York. While it's a given that tutors are typically doing other things, whether it's teaching, attending school, or working elsewhere, you want to find people who you feel will commit to at least several months consistently. Schwartz relays the story of a college student who wanted to work during the summer as a tutor, which would have been all right, except that she was going away at different times during the summer. On again/off again is not a good policy for any employee, much less one who is trying to build a relationship with students. With that in mind, you'll need to put policies in place regarding tutors leaving and returning. If, for example, you have some college students tutoring each summer, that can work, provided they can give you a chunk of time, such as seven consecutive weeks. Throughout the busier school year, you want to have a list of tutors that doesn't change very often, so that you can establish some steady tutor–student relationships that will last for the school year.

Of course, you may need to scout your competition if your turnover rate begins to rise and see what they're doing to keep their tutors on the payroll. Small incentives can work well, along with keeping up a competitive pricing structure. One thing that you may find cuts into your business is when a tutor starts working with a student through your business and then takes on the student on their own. You need to set up a policy up front that this is not allowed. Of course, you have little recourse, other than to stop using the tutor for other jobs. Again, don't assume people will just stick around. Make them part of your team by providing them with a sense of belonging. This comes from showing tutors respect, working with them to assess and help stu-

Bright Idea

While you may not be able to provide benefits, such as health insurance, you may be able to help tutors get lower rates by signing up for such plans as a group.

dents, and providing them with positive feedback, as well as perks and fair (competitive) wages, plus perhaps a bonus if their students meet their initial goals (passing a major exam, passing the course, etc.). As is always the case in business, you hold onto employees by treating them well. Listening to suggestions from your tutors and having occasional meetings (perhaps at a restaurant) for some brainstorming can keep everyone involved. Employees, whether full-time, part-time, or as independent contractors, feel a greater sense of ownership if they are included in the decision-making process.

Your Code of Ethics

Tutors, like teachers, need to uphold a code of ethics and maintain moral integrity in their work with students. While this may seem obvious, it's worth reviewing in light of questions that can be raised regarding what is and isn't appropriate.

And there's more than meets the eye. For example, how does a tutor respond if a student asks about other students with whom they are working? If a student talks to a tutor about other school issues, not related to coursework, how should a tutor respond? Can peer tutors get together socially outside of the tutoring session, since they are typically on the same college campus or in the same high school?

Yes, there are many possibilities, and as the owner of a tutoring and/or test prep business, you should have some guidelines in place for tutors and students to follow. In a competitive, litigious, and politically correct society, you must make sure that you and your tutors aren't opening any doors to trouble.

Ethical issues may also arise. One on-campus director of tutoring services explained the situation as it had applied to him. "Before commencing tutoring we were unfamiliar with the range of ethical issues facing a tutor. However, we were soon faced with situations of a sensitive nature. For example, a student approached one of us for another student's grade. To ensure confidentiality, we did not divulge the grade. Another ethical issue that arose was abandonment. It was important to not abandon students with emotional distress issues who came to see you when class was over. However, at the same time it was important to not neglect the next class of students waiting for tutorials to begin. To solve this issue we needed to be aware of appropriate avenues of assistance for student referral. For example, we could direct the student to the student counselor, academic skills adviser, or medical services staff. These ethical issues increased our awareness of and ability to cope with ethical issues." Organizations such as the Association for the Tutoring Profession (atp.jsu.edu) have their own codes of ethics. You can build yours around the following 10 concepts and concerns:

1. Contact between students and tutors is to be made through the tutoring facility, with the exception of phone calls to indicate that a tutor/student is running late or another such last-minute scheduling change.

2. Tutors must maintain strict confidentiality and privacy regarding grades, schoolwork, or other personal information about other students or tutors.

3. Tutors will be respectful and treat all students, parents, caregivers, and co-workers fairly and with dignity and respect regardless of race, ethnicity, culture, religion, gender, or socioeconomic background.

4. Tutors are obligated at all times to provide their best efforts to each and every student.

5. Tutors should limit any discussions not directly related to the work and study materials.

6. Tutors should never be alone with a student in a home or office facility. Another adult should be present in the home or facility during tutoring sessions.

7. Tutors should not make suggestive comments or those of a personal or sexual nature around students.

8. Tutors should not be under the influence of alcohol or non-prescription drugs or have any such items on them when tutoring.

9. There should be no physical interaction of any sort between a tutor and a student.

10. Tutors should not engage in any inappropriate activities or have any personal interaction with students.

The last one on the list can come into question in peer tutoring situations, since students attending the same high school or college are likely to see each other at other activities and may develop a social relationship. Similar to employees who work together and also have a social relationship, there should be a line drawn between the two relationships.

As an employer and business owner, the best you can do is to discuss these areas of concern with each tutor and draw up a code of ethics to be followed. You can have tutors sign that they have read and agree to the code and that you are not liable if they breach this agreement. While you would like all of your tutors to behave professionally at all times, one of your goals is also to run a reputable business to protect yourself should a questionable situation arise. By having tutors work in your facility, you can often limit potential problems that may arise when tutors are working in home environments.

Of course, the above ethical and moral guidelines also carry over to yourself and other non-tutors who are part of your staff. While most businesses are cautious regarding what's considered appropriate and inappropriate activity, tthere is a greater focus on teacher-student relationships today after stories such as that of a 28-year-old teacher who had a sexual relationship with a boy of 13.

While such incidents are by far the exception, it only takes one individual acting inappropriately (which can range from telling students dirty jokes to hugging to celebrate a good grade) to set your business back and cause a domino effect of cancellations.

Do your best to stay aware of your tutors' activities. If there is any report of inappropriate behavior, you will need to sit down with the parties involved and do your best to determine exactly what transpired. Tutors are not always the ones at fault. There are many stories of students acting inappropriately with tutors and stories that are also fictitious. Again, these are rare, but you need to be prepared to handle any such situation by gathering as many facts as possible and determining the best manner in which to settle a conflict, if one should arise.

Certification

While there are no laws in place nor any single governing body that says tutors must be certified, there are benefits that tutors gain by becoming certified. Since effective tutoring is not as easy as meets the eye, certification assures that the tutor has had some degree of training in the area of tutoring and has taken a serious approach to the endeavor. This can appeal to clients seeking tutors for their children, as well as to you as an employer. Anything you can do to enhance the credibility of your business and build a strong reputation for having highly skilled tutors is to your benefit.

There are a number of widely accepted certificate programs throughout the country, most of which stem from either tutoring associations or universities. With that in mind, some business owners have instituted a policy whereby all of their tutors are trained by the same program, such as the certification program offered by the National Tutoring Association (NTA), whose certification is designed to be earned at the individual or program level.

Typically, certification programs include a certain number of necessary hours committed to tutor training through classroom and workshop participation, training videos, online sources, written materials, or a combination of these and other means of disseminating information. Tutor responsibilities, guidelines, techniques, problem solving, and other necessary skills are taught, discussed, and/or reviewed in such certificate training programs.

Programs from which tutors can gain certification include:

- The College Reading and Learning Association offers national certification for tutors at crla.net.
- The International Tutoring Association offers high-quality training and certifi-

cation to all qualified tutors. Visit them at itatutor.org.

- The National Tutoring Association has a well-established tutor certificate program. You can find out about their program at ntatutor.com.

In most cases, tutors will find that certificate programs are relatively inexpensive, running under $100. Some will require that tutors renew their certification annually.

Stat Fact

In the past 20 years, the College Reading and Learning Association has provided tutor training certification to 300 college and university tutorial programs in the United States and Canada.

You can apply as a business to have all your tutors certified, or have tutors become certified on their own if you so choose. There is no law requiring certification; however, it is often a selling point, indicating that your tutors have been through some degree of formal training.

8

The Wide World of Tests and Test Prep

While most of this book talks about tutoring, the realities of hiring tutors and making sure they are skilled, reliable, trustworthy, and well versed in the ethics code discussed in the previous chapter are all applicable to the test prep business as well. This chapter is devoted exclusively to test preparation, which in recent years has become a fast-growing industry itself as competition for colleges and postgraduate programs becomes increasingly difficult.

Starting a test prep business means having practice tests on hand for each of the tests for which you offer help. It also means having skilled tutors who are one step ahead of the curve when it comes to:

- Understanding the tests

- Knowing how each test is scored

- Being able to explain proven strategies for achieving higher scores

Using a combination of notes from in-school review sessions, practice exams, and study guides designed for the individual exams, your test review courses should be able to cover each section of a given exam in a well-planned, well-paced course (or on a one-on-one basis) designed to culminate prior to the specific test. It's also important that you're on top of the scheduling for each of the tests for which you are providing classes and/or one-on-one tutoring. This will allow you to plan your courses and individual tutoring schedules accordingly.

Bright Idea

Have your tutors break tests down into their components. Most tests have several sections, some requiring different approaches and others focusing on different subjects. The SAT, for example, is divided into math, critical reading, and a writing component, as of a few years ago. By segmenting the exams, tutors can focus on the various portions of a test, making it easier (and less daunting) for students to study and prepare. You can also have separate tutors for specific areas if you choose, such as writing specialists for the SAT essays.

There are a number of well-known review courses and review books, particularly for the SAT, including those offered by Kaplan, Barron's, Ivy Insiders, Princeton Review, and even the makers of the actual test, The College Board. For your purposes, you might want to look at the websites for some of these established review courses and see what you can offer on a local, more personalized level, since it's unlikely that you will be able to compete with these larger entities for some years to come. Keep in mind that many smaller, local SAT, ACT, and other test prep businesses have gained popularity because they provide more personalized attention, direct answers, and individual assessment, which isn't always possible in the larger settings. In short, you are only as good as the successful students you produce.

Therefore, start small. After all, if you help 20 students and 18 do very well, your 90 percent success rate will have you growing more quickly than if you bite off more than you can chew by signing up 100 students and only helping 65 percent achieve higher scores. Word of mouth will be a major selling point if students do well and, in the course of their parents' bragging, they will tell the parents of next year's test takers where their son or daughter received such valuable help.

Test Prep Tutors

Being able to take a test and do well does not make for a good tutor. There's preparation that goes into being able to help students succeed on tests. A good tutor for test preparation needs to know how the students arrive at their answers and how they can arrive at the correct answer. Teaching and tutoring are about the process, not simply the answer. "Tutors needs to take time to familiarize themselves with the test so that if a students gets the question wrong they can find out how the student arrived at that answer," explains Hy Zamft, who, along with his wife, has run Zamft Tutoring from Katonah, New York for 16 years.

Being able to help each student find out what he or she did wrong and arrive at the right answer is one reason Zamft is not a fan of test prep classes, but instead feels the one-on-one approach is more beneficial. Zamft sometimes works with three students at once because he can still provide the personal attention they need, but finds that in the large classes some of the students won't get the attention they deserve. "You need to be able to provide something more, otherwise you are no different than a review book," adds Zamft. Neal Schwartz of the Tutoring Club has a similar outlook, and explains that they try to pair students with similar needs into groups of two or three. "Large classes go to the middle of the room and many students don't benefit," adds Schwartz, who has his students take the practice tests and then works with them on what they didn't know. "They can review the questions they got wrong and practice similar questions from other College Board–approved sample tests," explains Schwartz.

Test prep, particularly for the SAT and the ACT, is a significant part of most tutoring businesses. This is where you can make your money and build your reputation. Be careful, however, not to get greedy. Large classes from which you make more money but don't produce higher test scores can, in time, hurt your reputation.

> ⚠️ **Beware!**
> Since the format and structure of tests tend to change, make sure you're using the most recent and approved test samples. Contact the makers of the tests to make sure you're working with the latest sample tests.

The SAT

The most common test in prep courses is the SAT, which is taken by more than 2 million high school students annually as a means of providing colleges with a way to evaluate students for enrollment. Nearly 3,400 of the 4,100 colleges in the U.S. (or 80 percent) look at SAT scores and weigh them in their evaluation of individual students. As competition increases to get into the top colleges, the pressure to do well on the SATs also increases, with many students, and even more parents, hard pressed to make sure that scores are high. And that's where you come in. The test prep business is predicated on what has become a highly competitive environment.

The test, which was first given in 1926, was called the Scholastic Aptitude Test and was based on the concept of an I.Q. test, designed to measure intelligence and the innate ability of the student rather than strictly the lessons learned in school. Initially the test was to determine aptitude levels to show teachers which students were more likely to learn faster and which were more likely to need additional help.

In case you're wondering, the SAT prep business started shortly after the advent of the test itself, back in the late 1930s when Stanley H. Kaplan started tutoring students in his Brooklyn basement. Kaplan would go on to launch Kaplan Learning Centers, which today is a $2 billion business and continues to grow as the test is altered periodically, such as with the addition of a writing section in recent years. In fact, Andy Lutz, vice president for program development at the Princeton Review, was quoted as saying after the writing portion was added to the SAT a few years ago: "The fear and anxiety associated with changes in the SAT are good for our business."

Today, according to the College Board, the SAT is not designed to measure innate ability, but instead is a measure of developed reasoning, or so it has been explained by Wayne Camara, director of the office of research.

Some have criticized the SAT because preparation often can lead to much higher scores. The idea that those with more money can essentially buy their children 200 more points through prep courses is a major point of contention. However, your job is to simply provide a service for those who want it, and today that's the majority of the 2 million students who will take one of the upcoming SATs.

While the SAT has been shown to correlate well with first-year college performance, there has been little subsequent correlation regarding the remaining years of college or how well a student will do overall, as there are too many factors involved (i.e., course selection, major, social interactions, study habits, etc.).

The 2006–07 SAT report listed the national averages at 502 points in the critical reading section, 499 in the writing section, and 515 for mathematics. Your job in the test prep business is to raise those scores. In fact, some test prep businesses boast a 200-point increase, while most fall in the 50–150 range. Again, this will depend largely on the student's test-taking ability.

Whether you're personally involved in test preparation or supervising tutors who are heading up the SAT prep courses, your job as a business owner is to best prepare students to take this important exam, which means not only reviewing material, but providing effective strategies, improving writing skills, and teaching time management.

Using the model tests provided, since the actual tests have copyrights, an SAT tutor can work in conjunction with the practice tests (the PSATs) to help prepare students. Using the PSATs, and knowing where students are having difficulties allow a good tutor to prepare his or her focus and attention to help the student.

Schwartz and others favor studying for the PSAT, despite many schools saying, "Don't worry about it," in an effort to alleviate the pressure on students. Due to the lag time in getting results back from the PSATs, students who get poorer scores are then often stuck with little time to improve their skills for the SATs. However, if the student prepares and does well on the PSAT, the pressure will be lessened somewhat for the SAT, since the student will be equipped to take the test from early on. "Just taking a model PSAT can often improve a student's score by 100 points," adds Schwartz, who believes in starting early with the PSAT to avoid the last-minute SAT panic.

The SAT II

The SAT II tests are known as the subject tests and are also administered by the College Board, many typically given on the same day as the SAT I, or the more commonly known SAT test. These tests are designed to measure ability in a specific subject area and help a student further demonstrate his or her ability in a subject. For students looking to gain acceptance to certain college programs, these tests, along

Interesting Reading

Fair Test, The National Center for Fair and Open Testing points to several states that impose SAT minimum score requirements on students hoping to qualify for taxpayer-funded scholarships. Fair Test points out that the use of such cut-off scores to determine scholarships is a violation of the test-makers' guidelines. As a result, minority students, who tend to score lower on the SAT as a group than white students, receive fewer allocated scholarship dollars.

The Fair Test website, at fairtest.org, reports other gender and minority biases regarding the SATs and other tests. As an entrepreneur, it is worthwhile to know more about such discrepancies.

with the SAT I and good grades in specific subjects, can be beneficial. While the tests don't follow specific textbooks or curricula, they are designed to reflect the general high school curriculum.

The SAT II tests are offered in five general subject areas: English (literature), math, world history (including U.S. history), science (including biology, chemistry, and physics), and several languages. These tests are all one-hour, multiple-choice tests. For more on the SAT II subject tests, visit the College Board website at collegeboard.com.

The ACT

While the SAT has been around longer and has gained greater credibility on the east and west coasts, throughout much of the middle of the United States, the ACT has become the more common college entrance exam. Unlike the SAT, which focuses more on reasoning, problem-solving skills, and writing, the ACT is focused on book smarts based on the high school curriculum. Because of the difference in the exams, your tutors will focus more on fact-based answers, memorization, and a review of the in-class materials in various subjects for the ACT.

Since most, but not all, schools accept the ACT, students should know ahead of time which schools they are interested in and whether the ACT is the better test for them to take. For example, students with science-based career objectives who are looking for schools that specialize in that area can better show their strengths in that subject by taking the ACT. Students who do well in academic subjects but do not have the same strengths in reasoning ability will often do better with the ACT, while students who have a natural aptitude for solving problems may prefer to take the SAT.

Administered by the American College Testing Program, Inc., the ACT, which was first given in 1959, includes 215 questions in five sections: math, English, science, and reading. There is also an optional writing section. The highest score is 36, and the national average composite score in the United States for 2008 was 21.1. Roughly,

Bright Idea

While it's up to the student to decide between the SAT and the ACT, you can offer some counseling and advice on the subject that can set you apart from your competitors who are simply signing people up. Have a free consultation to determine which schools a student is interested in and talk with the student, parent, and tutor to help determine which test would be best for that student to take. While you're not serving as a college advisor, building a reputation for helping students make the right test choices (which can include when to take the PSAT, SAT, or ACT) can make you "the test prep business that cares."

only one in every 3,300 students gets a 36, or perfect score on the exam. Nearly 1.4 million American students took the ACT in 2008.

While time management is important for both the SAT and the ACT, the ACT has more questions to answer in a shorter time. Therefore, good tutors need to help with time management skills and strategies. Since students can select which ACT score they wish to send to colleges, they can be encouraged to take this test several times and work with a tutor between exams to cover areas in which they have difficulty.

Postgraduate Tests

Tests for postgraduate students are typically of an analytical nature. Tutoring is somewhat less frequent on a one-on-one basis, but classes are used for study and review purposes. At this point, you're dealing with students who have already demonstrated a high proficiency for learning and are career-driven. Since competition for business and law schools is fierce, you need experienced tutors who have "been there" and "done that," so to speak, before they start working with postgraduate students. Tutors need to know the exams backward and forward and be able to focus on areas of the exams as well as strategies.

The GRE

Developed by the Educational Testing Service (ETS) as a screening tool for graduate school applicants, the test, known as the Graduate Record Examination, has a scoring range from 200 to 800. The focus of the test is on abstract thinking and analytical writing, making it somewhat subjective and requiring tutors with proven abilities to work effectively in these areas.

The high-tech test is now computer-based, which has drawn some criticism as students cannot go back to a previous answer or skip a question, having to answer one before proceeding. It defies test-taking strategies for many students and also changes the level of difficulty as the student proceeds, which is subjective and has also drawn criticism. There are paper copies for certain areas where technology is lacking, but this is rare. Therefore, a tutor needs to be just as skilled at teaching the test-taking process of the GRE as at working on the material.

While the college entrance exams and the law school entrance exam (the LSAT) carry tremendous weight today, the GRE is received differently depending on the school and even the area of study. In many schools, the student's undergraduate GPA (grade point average) is as significant or more so than the GRE score. Nonetheless, for your purposes, you will want to have GRE-trained tutors available if you want to provide test prep in this area. ETS (ets.org) provides a book from which to study for

▲

the GRE as well as software called PowerPrep. Using these in conjunction with the tutoring you offer is advised.

The GMAT

The Graduate Management Admission Test® (GMAT) is a standardized assessment used by business schools to determine which applicants best qualify for graduate-level courses in business and management. The test is not designed to test specific knowledge of business or subject areas, but instead to measure math skills, verbal skills, and analysis of issues and arguments. The test was first introduced in 1953. Today, more than 200,000 students take it each year.

Scoring for the GMAT ranges between 200–800 with most people landing in the 400–600 range. Your tutors can help students add points to their scores by teaching them not only how to answer problems but by understanding the underlying principles for these kind of problems.

The LSAT

The Law School Admission Test (LSAT) is roughly a four-hour exam, including break time, that's required for admission by more than 200 law schools in the United States and Canada. The initial version of the LSAT was first given in 1948, but has changed considerably over the years. Administered four times annually by the Law School Administration Council, the test is divided into four sections, plus an unscored section where new questions are tested for future exams. Since the structure of the test remains the same from year to year and questions are similar, it allows tutors to work more effectively on reviewing the various sections and delving further into the process behind answering the questions, which includes logic, reasoning, and analytical reasoning.

Scoring for the LSAT ranges from 120–180. The test has 101 questions, and a raw score is calculated and then translated into the LSAT score. Unlike the SAT, which is weighed more evenly along with the student's high school grade average, the LSAT can count for 75-80 percent of a law school admissions board's criteria, the LSAT can carry up to 75 or 80 percent by law school admissions boards, making it "the" way in which to get into law school. Typically getting a score over 160 would land a student in one of the nation's top 25 law schools. For your purposes, you can charge upward of $1,200 for an eight-week LSAT course, higher than for any other exam prep course. Naturally you'll need a seasoned pro, with experience teaching law, to head such a course. Since getting 75 percent of the questions correct will typically put a student in the top 90th percentile, tutors can stress the idea of focusing on the questions with which the test taker is most comfortable and then going back to the others. Teaching LSAT test-taking strategies should be part of your tutors' repertoire.

Other Tests

Depending on the needs in your geographic area, you can offer other test preparation courses or tutoring sessions. When you spread the word that you have a test prep business (see Marketing in Chapter 11), you'll get inquiries about tests such as the Terra Novas for grade schoolers and the General Educational Development tests (GEDs) for American or Canadian high school equivalency. Since these and numerous other tests are based largely on curriculum through the high school level, it should be easier to find tutors locally who can handle this aspect of your business.

The same concept holds true with these tests as with the SATs or any other test prep. Make sure your tutors know the tests thoroughly, use the available practice tests and preparation books (if they exist), and have a grasp of the general subject matter that will be included. As is always the case with test prep, your tutors need to be able to explain why each answer is correct and how the student arrived at that answer. They should also know the strategies involved in performing well on the specific exam.

Other tests you can offer help with include:

ASVAB: The Armed Services Vocational Aptitude Battery is given to anyone considering joining the military.

ASWB: The Association of Social Work Boards are taken by anyone looking to earn a license in social work.

CAHSEE: The California High School Exit Examination is taken by all high school students in California. They must pass this exam to receive a diploma. Several other states have similar exams, such as the AHSGE (the Alabama High School Graduation Exam), which must be taken by high school students to receive a diploma.

CPAT: The Career Programs Assessment Test is given to students looking to attend a trade school.

DAT: The Dental Admission Test measures the knowledge and skills of individuals who are applying to dental school.

GED: The General Equivalency Diploma test is taken as a high school equivalency exam by nearly one million people a year to achieve the equivalent to their high school diploma.

HSPT: The High School Placement Test serves as a measure for private schools to assess and screen incoming high school students.

ISEE: The Independent School Entrance Exam is another test used as a measure of assessing and screening private school applicants.

MAT: The Miller Analogy Test is given for graduate school admissions.

MCAT: The Medical College Admissions Test is used for applying to medical schools.

NCLEX-RN: The National Council Licensure Examination-Registered Nurse is a test for becoming a certified RN.

NET: The Nursing Entrance Exam is used to screen applicants for nursing schools.

OAT: The Optometry Admission Test is taken by applicants to optometry programs.

PCAT: The Pharmacy College Admission Test is, as the name would suggest, given to applicants to pharmacy programs/colleges.

Praxis: The Praxis I exam is an initial teacher certification test. The Praxis II test focuses on measuring knowledge and skills within various content areas.

These are some of the multitude of tests that exist. Find out what students need to take in the state or states in which you will be doing business. You can do well with state-mandated, high school–level exams, such as the many Regents' tests given in individual subjects in the state of New York or the state tests given in California, Alabama, Tennessee, and elsewhere for high school students to get their diplomas. Mandatory tests create anxiety and you can provide a much-needed solution.

Also, remember that using preparation books in conjunction with tutoring is the optimal way to help students, since this allows you to see actual practice materials and test questions, plus it gives the student a means of discussing and evaluating what he or she got wrong by working with the tutor.

Hiring for Test Prep

Not unlike hiring for any type of academic tutoring, you are seeking individuals who are good communicators, good listeners, and enthusiastic about the subject matter and educating their students. In addition, familiarity with and proficiency in the specific tests is a must. The more comfortable the tutor is with the test material and the types of questions that will be asked and necessary strategies, the more confident the students will be … and confidence is a big part of test preparation and test taking.

9

Starting an Online Tutoring Business or Buying a Tutoring Franchise

Two of the most popular means of starting a business today are starting a web-based online business and buying a franchise.

Both of these are feasible ways to launch a business, although very different. Web-based businesses can be started for little upfront money and run at a fairly low cost. They pro-

▲

vide you with far-reaching opportunities. Launching a website is not difficult today, and with so many available web designers, your site can look great without spending a fortune. The problem is generating business through marketing. Since you're part of the extensive World Wide Web and don't have a brick-and-mortar location where people can drop by or see your sign, you must find ways to build a customer base from scratch.

Conversely, franchises are a more costly means of starting up a business, requiring significant upfront money, with plenty of cash on hand. However, they typically come with ready-made promotion and, in most cases, a recognition factor that would take years to build from scratch. In this chapter we'll look at both of these popular, yet contrasting, means of starting your business.

Online Tutoring

There are several positive features about starting an online tutoring business. First, you can start from a homebased office and work in your pajamas if you choose. This allows you to save a bundle on overhead, other than the costs of updating and maintaining the latest interactive computer technology.

Essentially, the requirements from a technical standpoint are fairly basic. A broadband connection at a minimum of 128 kB per second, a headset microphone, and a good speaker, plus voice chat capabilities, are the basics. A camera for face-to-face communication is also an option. Online whiteboards can be used to allow students and tutors to write, draw, or provide means of visualizing materials, as well as posting lessons. Of course, instant messaging and e-mail, as well as discussion boards, are all commonly used means of online communication between tutors and students.

The technology is all available through a skilled web designer, or you can do it yourself using software from places like esitesbuilder.com or websites-now.net. You can also visit onlinetutoringworld.com for more details on building a homebased online tutoring business. The point is, there is plenty of information available on building a website. More significantly, you need to determine how you plan to make the business work and how you will market it, as discussed in Chapter 11 on marketing.

Online tutors send and receive written questions and answers, send and receive quizzes, send quiz results and recommendations, teach concepts, analyze material, and handle the same tasks as an in-person tutor. Students can either interact live with the tutor or have material sent back and forth and completed at the student's own pace.

You will need to envision the way you want your tutors to interact with students. In real time, you will have to have tutors ready during a specific time frame to field questions and work with students. Another option is to post materials and have students sign in with password protection to get the work and do the assignments, or take exams and hand them in to be graded and/or reviewed and then returned to the students. Whether or not you use video, some form of live interaction (which could be as simple as IMs back and forth) seems to be the most popular method today.

The Debate: Online Tutoring vs. Traditional (In-Person) Tutoring

Obviously, the advantages of one-on-one in-person tutoring are body language, looks and gestures, and the nuances that make up such person-to-person communication. It's easier to establish a rapport when two people are in the same place at the same time. Nonetheless, online tutoring has grown by leaps and bounds in recent years. Starting up such a business isn't difficult and scheduling can be easier for you as a business owner, since the tutor and student don't need to incorporate travel time into the process. Here are some pros and cons to the basic process that is online tutoring.

The Pros of Online Tutoring

- You can run the business from a home office.
- From a business perspective, you can market your services to a larger audience, since geographic region isn't a factor.
- From a business perspective, the number of potential tutors is much broader.
- If tutors aren't only working in real-time situations, they can interact with students at any time. For example, a student can send a paper in at midnight and the tutor can grade it at some point during the next day.
- The use of portable computers and handheld devices allows for interaction to take place out of the home or tutoring facility ... from just about anyplace.
- Students and tutors can draw from a large volume of online resources, which are at their fingertips.
- If you have a setup with tutors available regularly, students can get questions answered at any hour of the day or night.
- Inclement weather, transit delays, or congested roadways won't throw off the time of a tutoring session.
- It's easy to review tutoring sessions by saving them for future reference.

The Cons of Online Tutoring

- Valuable in-person, face-to-face interaction is missing, and conversations lose something in the communication process.

- E-mail and IM remarks and comments can be misconstrued.

- For students who work best in controlled environments, online tutoring is not always effective, since there is less structure and the tutoring process can be taking place from anywhere.

- Not everyone has the same level of internet service. Signals get lost and servers go down. Technology can interfere with communications.

- From a business point of view, it can be harder to establish the credibility of an online tutor whom you may not have met in person.

- Students can get outside help with work before sending material to the tutor. While the student is essentially hurting himself or herself, the tutor won't be aware of it, since he or she isn't witnessing the student actually doing the work.

- Students (and tutors) may not be paying 100 percent attention to the session.

Setting It Up as You See Fit

The effectiveness of online tutoring will be largely based on how you set up the process. For example, TutorVista.com has students book specific blocks of 45 minutes with a tutor (tutorvista.com). Then there's Tutor.com, where tutors are available day or night in all core subjects from fourth grade through high school (tutor.com).

However you set up your online tutoring, you'll need a simple, yet efficient process of payment, which can be through billing or payment of x amount in advance for x amount of time. For example, you might decide that at $40 an hour, a student can buy five hours for $200 and then take a half-hour session if he or she so chooses. You might throw in one half-hour free as a promotion. You could also have time logged on and off and the student could use up the hours in any time segment, which would allow them to call in for answers to questions when they're stuck. Another option might be to have several students paying in advance and signing up to attend an online tutoring session at a specified time.

There are a number of ways in which you can set up online tutoring. The key is to have:

- Some available options

- Web-savvy tutors

- A secure way to receive payment

You'll also want to have a means for parents to communicate with your business and receive regular updates on the progress of their child. One mom tells a story of her daughter becoming a "chat buddy" with one of the tutors. The company refunded some of the money and explained to the tutor that this was a waste of the time for which the parent is paying money.

This, of course, brings us to the issue of what is and is not permissible. Again, as is the case in any tutoring situation, guidelines must be clear. Often, the anonymity of

> **Beware!**
> Make sure you have a privacy policy written up and read by your clients before they sign up. Also include rules about passwords being used by only one person. While you cannot completely monitor who is using the password on the other end, you can alert your tutors to be aware of suspicious activity. Online tutors have become suspicious in many instances of other people signing on under a client's password and using their tutoring time. The better the tutors know the students with whom they work, the less likely it is that someone can pose as that student.

the internet encourages people to say things they might not say to someone in person. You need to monitor your tutors to avoid such situations.

Additionally, while tutors save travel time, they'll need to take the time and effort to know the technology and means of communicating very well, which will sometimes mean preparing material and posting it in advance of a session or class.

Your goal or mission, as an online tutoring service provider, will factor into how you set up your business. If you're focused on test preparation, then you may be better off setting up specific scheduled time frames in which real-time test activities, such as practice exams or test strategies, can take place. However, if you're coaching and helping with day-to-day homework and weekly test/quiz preparation, then you might opt for the "call anytime" approach where short answers and discussions are more frequent. However, you should notify parents and students ahead of time that tutors will help them find answers, which may take two or three minutes, rather than giving them the answer in 30 seconds, which is not as beneficial to the student (although it saves money). The objective is to tutor and not become the "answer guys," which won't help the students on tests.

Your hope is that your tutors can provide guidance, instruction, and feedback in an interactive manner, allowing students to ask questions, show or explain their work, and make it clear in which areas they are seeking help.

Franchises

Franchising means buying into an existing larger company and using their name and know-how to start your own business. From a startup perspective, it's a way to jump into the pool rather than going in step by step. The business is already established, so you need not reinvent the wheel. Of course, the down side of a "ready-made" business is the cost. Franchises can be costly.

Before going into the pros and cons of franchising, it's worth noting that three of *Entrepreneur* magazine's top 150 franchises for 2008 (from a larger list of the top 500) are in the tutoring/education industry. First you'll find the ever-popular Sylvan

▲

A Dozen Steps to Starting an Online Tutoring Business

1. Decide what subjects you'll offer, for what age range, and how you'll structure the online service. Pay by the hour? Sign up for x number of hours? Pay for a week? A month?
2. Establish your hourly rates(s) for multiple sessions.
3. Set up a website; you can do it yourself or use the help of a web designer.
4. Do an online search through the multiple software possibilities and decide which one best suits your needs.
5. Design, post your information on your website, and test it to make sure everything works. Redesign the look of the site until you're happy with the results.
6. Before launching your site, make sure you have credit card accessibility and a Paypal account (paypal.com) or another means of collecting payment.
7. Before launching your site, make sure you have an 800 number in place.
8. Before launching your site, make sure you have a privacy policy and any contractual agreements that you'll need ready and reviewed by an attorney.
9. Before launching your site, hire the appropriate number of tutors for the subjects and hours you'll offer.
10. In conjunction with launching your online tutoring business, advertise and promote your new business heavily. Remember, do your research so you'll get the most bang for your advertising buck.
11. Launch your site and promptly field all inquiries via e-mail or telephone. Offer an introductory discount or free consultation, if necessary.
12. Sign up students, follow up closely on results from (or monitor) tutor–students interactions, and stay abreast of payments. Continuously update the website and make sure all functions are in working order. Have technical support handy at all times.

Learning Centers, the most successful tutoring franchise in the country, franchising since 1980. The Baltimore-based franchise business not only has learning centers in the United States, but also in Asia. To qualify for a Sylvan franchise, you will need to have a net worth of at least $250,000 and $75,000 cash liquidity. The total investment, including a $40k–48k franchise fee, will run roughly between $180k and $300k. There is an ongoing royalty fee of 8–9 percent and the renewable franchise agreement is for 10 years.

While Sylvan does not require an education background, it does help. Business, marketing, and industry experience are typical requirements for Sylvan and most educational franchises. Training is only one week at the company headquarters plus five days at a regional location and at the franchisee's grand opening. One plus is that it only takes a few people to run a Sylvan franchise. The big plus, however, about Sylvan is the recognizable name and franchise history of success. Additionally, you'll have a newsletter, website, and toll-free phone number, plus plenty of marketing support in terms of advertising in national media.

The second most successful U.S. tutoring franchise listed on *Entrepreneur*'s annual top 500 is Huntington Learning Centers, Inc. For 24 years, the New Jersey–based franchise has been growing throughout the country, and it is still actively seeking new franchisees for a total investment running between $203k and $394k, including the $43k franchise fee. Similar to Sylvan, a net worth of $250,000 is a requirement, with $60,000 in cash liquidity. Huntington requires an ongoing royalty fee of 8 percent, a 10-year contract, and a renewal fee of $20,000. A four-week training program at headquarters and at various locations (a couple of times a year) is also required. Support is similar to that given by Sylvan, including the newsletter, website, toll-free phone line, and so on. National television advertising is a plus, along with other advertising and marketing support.

The third educational/tutoring business to find its way into *Entrepreneur*'s highly regarded Top 500 franchises, also in the top 150, is Club Z. Much newer, Club Z began franchising in 1998 from its home base in Tampa, Florida. While Club Z doesn't have the immediate name recognition of Sylvan or the national television budget of Huntington, it is more affordable for the newcomer looking to launch a business. The total investment is in the $32k to $65k range with only a $25,000 cash liquidity qualification. Royalty fees are at 6 percent and the franchise agreement is renewable in seven years. One of the biggest advantages of a Club Z franchise for a new entrepreneur is that it is a franchise that can be run from home, which also explains the much lower franchisee cost.

The biggest advantage of a franchise, as noted earlier, is the instant recognition factor, which makes marketing and advertising that much easier. In addition, with sufficient support and guidance, a franchisee shouldn't have to reinvent the wheel, since most franchises have a working system in place for running the business. The benefit is that, despite the bigger investment in most cases, franchise owners don't have to wait nearly as long to see a steady stream of income, since the business is jump-started.

Of course, not everyone will want to go the franchise route. If playing by someone else's rules doesn't appeal to you as a business owner, if you are intent on establishing your own brand and doing things your own way, you may not be a prime candidate for a tutoring franchise. While there is some flexibility and you're in charge, franchises have established ways of doing things and they have been proven effective in the successful ones. The degree to which you can "do it your way" will vary depending on the franchise. For those who prefer some guidance and structure, a franchise is a great way to launch a business without much trial and error. As one franchisee put it, "There is a comfort zone, which is not found when you start a business from scratch."

Do Your Homework

While a tutoring business helps students handle their homework, you'll need to do

> **Stat Fact**
> With minimal searching, particularly on the internet, you'll also find other tutoring franchises among the more than 6,000 franchise opportunities in the United States. The popularity of franchising is as hot as ever, with business owners opening up new franchises at a rate of nearly 300 per week.

yours before buying a franchise. "There are a lot of franchise companies out there where the franchisor makes a lot of money and does very well and the franchisees just sort of struggle and get by," explains Eric Stite, founder and president of Franchise Business Review (franchisebusinessreview.com), a company designed to help prospective franchisees determine whether a franchise is right for them, based on franchisee satisfaction surveys.

While the better franchises make money from successful franchisees, there are some that leave owners high and dry. Therefore, knowing what kind of support the franchise will provide is important. Stite also stresses the importance of talking to franchisees to get the inside track on how good the franchise opportunity really is.

The key is doing your homework, learning as much as possible about the franchise, and reading the franchise agreement carefully (and having it reviewed by your attorney before signing). The franchise agreement outlines the expectations and requirements of the franchisor and describes its commitment to the franchisee. The agreement should also include information about the territorial rights of the franchisee, as well as the training offered, the fees, the general obligations of each party, and so on.

The Pros of Buying a Tutoring Franchise

- **Proven Business:** A franchise is a business that has been proven to operate successfully and generate a profit. It takes a lot of the guesswork out of starting your own business.

- **Established Brand and Customer Base:** A huge positive for buying a franchise is that it has the strength of brand name recognition and a reputation.

- **Franchise Support:** A good franchise should provide a lot of business support in the way of training and problem solving. You're not alone when you become part of a franchise

- **Financial Assistance:** Many franchises provide financial assistance. Also, if you need to apply to a lending institution for a loan, it's typically easier when you're using the money for a proven franchise than starting your own business from scratch.
- **Quick Start:** You can get the business off the ground more quickly.

The Cons of Buying a Tutoring Franchise

- **High Cost:** Some franchises cost a substantial amount of money upfront, more than you would likely need to start on your own business.
- **Royalty Payments:** You will be paying part of your profits to the franchise company, typically anywhere from 5–10 percent.
- **Limits to Your Freedom and Creativity:** Franchises are typically run in a fairly standard manner, leaving you with less freedom and limiting your creativity.
- **Fees:** There are usually marketing and advertising fees associated with owning a franchise.
- **Long-Term Contracts:** Typically the franchise agreement is for 8–10 years.

Stat Fact
According to AZFranchises.com, there are 1,500 franchises in the United States, with over 750,000 locations and 18 million employees. For more franchise statistics, check out azfranchises.com/franchisefacts.htm.

Plenty of Places to Look

As franchising becomes increasingly popular and more entrepreneurs consider going that route, the number of resources available continues to grow. Franchise Business Review, mentioned earlier, is an excellent place to gather franchisee enthusiasm about specific franchise opportunities. You can also gain valuable information at Entrepreneur.com's franchise section from entrepreneur.com/franchises/index.html.

Other places to learn about franchising include:

- Frandata at frandata.com
- Bison Franchise & Business Opportunities at bison.com
- The American Franchise Association at franchisee.org
- The International Franchise Association at franchise.org
- *Franchise Times* magazine at franchisetimes.com
- *US Franchise News* at usfranchisenews.com

In the end, whether you opt to start your own online tutoring business, go the franchise route, or seek out your own location, as a new business owner you'll need to have your own website (although franchises generally provide them), as well as the tools of the business trade for your office and for your tutors.

An important part of setting up any business today is making sure that you have the necessary communication tools, equipment, and technology to stay abreast of what's going on in your industry and the world around you. In addition, you'll want to be on the cutting edge when it comes to ways in which to promote and market your business. All of these areas will be the focus of the next two chapters.

Technology and the Tools of the Trade

Today, nearly every business has a website, and your tutoring and/or test prep business should be no exception. A professional website, created with the help of a skilled web designer, is a necessary part of doing business today.

There are three main purposes for having a website.

1. You can promote the type of tutoring and classes you offer, list your prices, and provide information about your business.

2. You can use the site as a means of signing up students for tutoring sessions, joining classes, and/or attending seminars if you offer them as well.

3. You can use the website as an interactive means of disseminating information through online tutoring (as mentioned in the previous chapter) and/or as a supportive tool for your tutors to provide classwork, offer discussion boards, post blogs entries, and offer other means of communication.

Any or all of these uses of a website can prove significant for your business.

Designing Your Website

It's always advised that a new business owner look at the sites of other businesses to get an idea of the look that he or she wants for the website. While you can't take someone else's content, you can look at the layout and the color combinations used on a wide range of sites to determine what best suits your purposes.

Since you're in the education business, you'll want to have a design and an image that looks "smart," and perhaps scholarly, without looking stuffy. Sites like Kaplan, Sylvan, Tutoring Club, and Club Z all have children of different ages on uncluttered, well-centered pages with some color and easy navigation through a few key links to areas such as Higher Education, Test Prep, Reading & Math, Location, About Us, and so on.

The look of the site needs to reflect your business and be consistent from page to page. It needs to be user-friendly, meaning it's easy to find a few key sections on which to click. White space is not a bad thing on a web page, as it affords the page visitor the opportunity to focus on the important information rather than having to search the screen for it.

While looking at other websites, save those that appeal to you in terms of style and layout to show your site designer. Be careful in your use of color. Some bright colors may show up poorly on other users' screens. Also a colorful print on a colorful background can be hard to read on handheld devices and smaller screens. You should also avoid those clever hard-to-load graphics—they're energy wasters (in an age of energy conservation) and they load slowly, prompting visitors to go elsewhere. The amount of business lost on people who don't want to wait for fancy web graphics to load is staggering.

The Important Web Pages

The look of your site is only half of the equation. Your website needs to include pages that provide your viewers with information, whether it's the subjects in which you offer tutoring, the states in which you are located, the tests for which you offer test prep, or all of the above. You want everything to be reader-friendly, concise, and effective, meaning that you're selling while informing. Take the opportunity to include content centered around learning and education. For example, write about what parents should look for in a good tutor or provide tips for making tutoring effective for young children. As a new entity, you need to demonstrate that you know as much about the business as the big players and that you provide the latest in teaching methods with top-notch tutors. Also, focus on your competitive edge. Whatever you can provide that your competition doesn't is your competitive edge, whether that means lower prices or e-mail follow-ups with personalized attention.

From a technical standpoint, it's important that all pages link to the information the user is seeking. Don't make visitors to your website jump hurdles to find what they're looking for or they'll give up.

Typically, your page links will include:

- Subjects offered
- Locations served
- Your general teaching philosophy (individual learning styles, a specific learning plan, etc.)
- Test prep offered
- Prices and how to sign up (if you are signing up students online, you'll need the necessary software)
- About Us (this is an important section, explaining who you are and how you came to run a tutoring business)
- Privacy page (have a lawyer review this page)
- Contact Us (a must for any commercial website)

You should consider having content and even some interactive sections including polls, surveys, and other ways in which viewers can get involved. Some websites have a place for tutors to sign up if they're interested in joining your company. Another popular page is an FAQ page, where you answer the most frequently asked questions. Since you are a new business, you'll have to assume what people will be asking and provide the popular Q&A format.

Make sure your page is current and update the content often. Also, if you include reciprocal links to/from other businesses, make sure you check out the other businesses carefully before accepting a link. Remember, your credibility is very important. If you're signing up students online, make sure you have an easy sign-up procedure. If students need to ask questions, respond within 24 hours with the necessary information.

▲

Maintain Your Website

Links break and content gets stale. How often do you look at a website in October and see a schedule for September classes or a deadline that has passed? Don't let this happen to you. Maintaining your website is essential to business in the internet age. This includes checking to see that links go to the pages with which they are supposed to connect.

You will likely need someone with technical knowledge to help you maintain your site, so seek out some good technical help in your neighborhood. While you don't want to have a wealth of pages, you should add pages for anything new to your business, such as an exam or a promotion.

Computers and Office Equipment

Computers are essential to nearly all businesses today. While you will need to purchase the appropriate software for your purposes, having the right computers will make running your business easier, allowing you to use programming and scheduling software, as well as using educational programs if and when you choose to support your efforts.

Computer shopping for a small business is not much different than personal computer shopping. You need to have enough speed and power to handle the programs, while also feeling comfortable with your choice of computer, since you'll be using it every day.

Computer Needs

If you don't already have one, or if your current one has morphed into a dinosaur, buying a computer system will be high on the list of startup expenses. For a basic system—hard drive, monitor, mouse, modem, printer—allocate anywhere from $800 to $2,500, depending on your needs. Many people today are opting for notebook computers over desktops for several reasons.

Notebooks are portable, take up minimal space, and use less energy than desktops (they are essentially greener). The downside, however, is that they are also easier to drop and break (or lose data) or have stolen. Additionally, some people are more comfortable with the larger screen and mouse that the desktop provides. The choice is yours ... many businesses have at least one of each.

Computer Specs

Your computer will be the command center of your office setup. What should you look for in a computer system? Here are some minimum requirements:

- Pentium or other fast processor
- Current version of Microsoft Windows
- 2-4 GB RAM
- 120-320 GB hard drive
- DVD +/- RW
- Broadband connection
- At least two universal USB connections for peripherals, which will typically include your printer and perhaps a scanner (most desktop computers come with four USB ports—more are definitely better)
- Windows Aero-capable graphics card and 128 MB of graphics memory (minimum)

You can always acquire more. For example, while 1 GHZ is the minimum recommended speed, having over 2 GHZ for laptops (a compromise to avoid excessive battery drain) or 3 GHZ for desktops is advisable to get a snappier response. If it's networking you want, or need with several in-office computers for your tutors, the new and improved Vista Home and Vista Business work with two kinds of networks. Only Vista Ultimate can be used with either a peer-to-peer (usually five or fewer PCs) or central server (big company) kind of network.

A computer meeting the above standards should be able to handle anything you as a tutoring entrepreneur should need. There are, however, plenty of bells and whistles that can be included. Keep in mind that you shouldn't spend more, or waste additional energy, on features you don't need. Determine your computer needs and uses in advance.

Speed is important when using the Internet or trying to bring up data while talking to a client on the phone. With a good computer as your silent partner, you can:

- Create and maintain a schedule for your tutors and students
- Maintain student progress data
- Maintain the latest tests
- Create marketing brochures, display ads, and even direct mail pieces
- Generate stationery, invoices, and business forms
- Maintain your books
- Perform accounting functions and generate financial reports
- Access research materials and other resources online

▲

- Maintain data and background materials on your current tutors and new applicants
- Do a wealth of marketing, which can include an online newsletter

Printers

For your purposes, you will probably opt for speed over color graphic quality. With that in mind, a good laser printer should suffice. Laser printers are faster and more durable than their inkjet counterparts. Your printing needs will probably include basic flyers, materials for students, and contracts. For around $350 you should be able to find a printer that will meet your needs. If you are environmentally conscious, as most of your customers will be, you should consider buying a printer with recycled parts. HP and other leading printer manufacturers are now using recycled plastics in their products.

Also, in the green mode of thinking, you should only print what you need and whenever possible use both sides of the page, saving on paper. Buying recycled paper is also advised.

As with computers, printers have a host of features. Again, look for the features you need and not the ones that will simply bring the price up.

Bright Idea

The two primary places to shop for computers are at manufacturers' websites and major big box retailers such as Best Buy or PC Richard. In either case, look to purchase an extended warranty. The extra expense will usually be worth it.

Smart Tip Tip...

Buy a surge protector to protect against a power outage that could potentially wipe out the files you're working on. You can also opt for a UPS (uninterruptible power supply) which is even better than a surge protector because it serves as a short-term backup generator for the computer, letting you continue to work for several minutes, closing and/or backing up the files you're working on.

Software Skinny

Software for the tutoring and test prep business is necessary for organization, scheduling, time management, bookkeeping, accounting, and data maintenance on tutors and students. Of course, there are numerous programs available. Intuit's Home & Business 2008 (quicken.intuit.com), among a variety of other programs, can handle most of your needs. You'll find other software reviewed at websites like ZDNet.com (zdnet.com), *Business Software Review* (businesssoftwarereview.com), and *PC Magazine* (pcmag.com). Intuit QuickBooks or Microsoft Money can help you track your business finances, while a host of project management programs can help you keep everything organized. Visit project-management-software.org for some options. Programs like Schedule It Pro 4 and When to Work are highly rated for scheduling, and Dovico's TimeSheet is a popular choice for time tracking and management purposes.

Your goal is to find the most easily compatible software to make your job easier. Don't opt for elaborate software if it means you'll be spending too much time on the learning curve. The best software is the one that lets you hit the ground running, so to speak, or is user-friendly *for you*.

Laurie Hurley, owner of Home Tutoring Business, decided that it was time for the tutoring business to have an accounting program of its own. Hurley, who oversees 60–70 tutors working with more than 200 students, hired a programmer to write the program for her and the end result was Accounting Tools for Tutors (accounting-toolsfortutors.com). "There are other good programs, but they are not set up for tutoring with its many nuances," explains Hurley, who wanted to fulfill the needs of the industry.

The internet-based, password-protected program allows the business owner to use it from any location, so traveling is not a problem. "The program lets you see everything that is going on. People cancel and reschedule for another day, clients want to know exactly when the tutor came and what they are being billed for, and tutors want to know how much they will make for the hours they put in. Therefore, the program is designed for accounting, contact management, record keeping, maintaining profiles of tutors and students, making payments, issuing credits when necessary, phone numbers and contacts, and so on," explains Hurley of her tutoring-specific program.

The last "must have" on your software list is an antivirus program. Often, you can have one loaded onto your computer when you buy it, as part of the package. Bit Defender, PC-cillin, Panda Antivirus, McAfee Virus Scan, AVG Antivirus Pro, and Norton Antivirus are all leading brands, and you *need* to have one on your computer before you even think of hooking up with the internet. Viruses are rampant in cyberspace and you're jeopardizing your entire business if you don't protect your computer. Just as you lock your doors and close your windows when you leave your home, you need to ensure that your computer is secure. Also, remember to update the antivirus software frequently because new threats are constantly circulating as hack-

Smart Tip

Make sure you have your essential software for starters, which includes:

- Windows (current version)
- A user-friendly accounting software program
- Some type of scheduling program, which could even be a basic Excel spreadsheet if you like
- Antivirus (very important)

ers continue to play the role of cyberspace villain.

Furnishing Your Facility

If you're working from a home base, you can go with secondhand furnishings and garage sale goodies. If, however, you have a facility from which your tutors and students will be working, you'll need to furnish accordingly.

In a dedicated tutoring facility, you'll want to set up the space so that a few tutoring sessions can take place at once

Smart Tip

Besides a variety of dedicated whiteboard software programs, keep in mind that Google and Adobe offer free systems that allow online collaboration and sharing of documents (but not the whole desktop). Microsoft offers its own Sharepoint software system for document collaboration. Also, the Take-Me-to-My-PC company offers a shared desktop system for demonstrations and meetings with a 30-day free trial.

without interfering with each other. This may mean dividers if there are no separate rooms. It also means spreading out the tutoring areas and making sure that each space gets adequate ventilation and proper lighting. One of the most important, and often overlooked, factors in any business setting is good lighting, and it doesn't necessarily mean fluorescent lights, which not only use up a lot of electricity but give some people headaches. You want overhead lighting that covers the room(s), but more importantly, task lighting so that there are lamps or other available lights for reading and working on projects, as needed. For your purposes, you should also opt for LED and/or CFL bulbs. While these bulbs may cost a little more than the traditional bulbs, both will be cost-effective down the road because they will last significantly longer. An LED bulb has a lifespan of 60,000 hours, while a CFL bulb can keep going for 10,000 hours, significantly more than the 1,500 hours for most energy-hog incandescent bulbs.

Desks need not be elaborate, but should have a new look and be functional for students and tutors to share. Tables may provide even more space. Chairs should also be functional and comfortable enough for learning, but not too comfortable.

While the space need not have an elaborate décor, you want to present a highly functional setting that's appealing. For younger students, such as new readers, you'll want to have an area with some color and kid-friendly furnishings to spark their enthusiasm.

Make sure that all computer wiring and any other technology is safely out of the way of young children. In addition, review your space carefully for potential hazards including chipped paint, lead paint, loose floorboards or ceiling panels, or anything else that could be a disaster in the making. The traffic flow should be unencumbered in the work areas. If you're using some type of dividers, make sure they, too, are safely in place.

Whiteboards and chalkboards are typically part of a learning facility, as are the many books that accompany a tutoring and test prep business. You may elect to have one specific area where bookshelves are found so that everyone knows where the books belong and they don't end up as potential hazards all over your facility or disappear.

If you're looking to maintain greenness in your tutoring location, you might opt to shop at The Green Office (thegreenoffice.com), where you can get many eco-friendly alternatives for supplies and furniture. For workstations and tables, you might also take a look at EcoWork (ecowork.com). Maintaining a green office space also means keeping a close eye on the cleaning materials you use, opting for non-toxic cleaning fluids and those that don't create indoor air pollution. Many of these products are non-toxic, biodegradable, and made from renewable resources (not petroleum).

Finally, regarding furnishing your tutoring facility, you want to look for discounts on furniture when buying in bulk. For example, six $150 workstations might be negotiated to $750 rather than $900. While you want furnishings that look clean and new, focus more on function over form. After all, neither the kids nor their parents will focus on the furnishings unless something looks out of place or dilapidated.

Phone Systems

The first rule of thumb when buying a telephone system is simply don't buy more than you need. Stories abound of small businesses with multi-line complex (intimidating) telephone systems that require a short course just to use them.

Don't become one of those businesses that, thanks to a fast-talking salesperson, has a complex phone system that nobody is comfortable using. Instead, consider the number of people, the amount of telephone business you anticipate (some businesses are largely based on internet communications), and then determine what's practical for your business. A homebased tutoring business can likely survive with a good two-line phone, a good voice mail service (answering machines sound amateurish), and, of course, your handy cell phone.

Since most, if not all, of your tutors will also have their handy cell phones, you need no longer accommodate everyone who works for you with a phone. Since you need to have broadband today in the fast-paced world of the internet, you won't need a separate phone line any longer for dial-up service.

Phones become more expensive with the additional features. Determine what best suits your needs. Then, shop around for a good deal, especially for your cell phone. Everyone wants your business, so don't jump at the first deal you see. Verizon, Sprint, T-Mobile, Nextel, AT&T, and others are all offering various deals. Compare and decide. You can compare phone plans online at websites, including CNET. (cnet.phonedog.com/cell-phone-research/compare-plans.aspx).

Your Library

Inside the homes of tutoring business owners, or in their offices, you'll see a great number of books. Having these handy resources, despite the wonders of the internet, is a plus for your business and looks good for your credibility and your reputation as a learning provider.

Along with the test guides for every test for which you offer preparation, you should have some of the basics, including a dictionary, thesaurus, and some textbooks in various subjects. You'll want to get a list of the textbooks used in the schools in your immediate area and have available as many as you can, since students will often forget to bring along the right books. There are also some general guides to colleges, such as the *Best 361 Colleges* from the Princeton Review Board or the *Fiske Guide to Colleges* from Sourcebooks, that are good to have on hand, plus guides to private schools, graduate schools, and law schools (if you are doing LSAT prep work). While you're not serving as a college planner, advisor, or consultant, you can help by having such references available to answer basic college questions.

Additional Needs

Office supplies are always necessary. Consider green alternatives when possible. Make a list of what you'll need for office use and try to keep tabs on supplies that have a tendency to walk away.

As for printing, what you can't do in your office, you can have done by professional printers. Business cards may be of a higher quality from a professional printer than from a software program, although some software programs do a pretty good job. You want business cards for yourself and for your tutors. Recycled paper and soy ink can look just as good as any other business cards while benefiting the environment. Shop around for printing needs and compare prices.

Other needs will depend on the size of your facility and number of tutors you have. Remember, if you're working from a home office you can keep a list of your business expenses and deduct your business expenses on your tax return. You can also deduct the proportion of your home expenses dedicated to business. For example, when paying your mortgage or paying rent, you can deduct the percentage of your space used exclusively for business. Therefore, if you home is 2,500 square feet and your office and storage space dedicated for work is 250 square feet, you can deduct 10 percent of your mortgage or rent payments as business deductions. The same holds true when driving your personal vehicle to meet tutors or students. The amount of mileage used for business can be deducted based on that which is allowable by the IRS (irs.gov).

The Fine Art of
Marketing Your
Business

Marketing means different things to different business owners. For some it involves a full-scale marketing plan that encompasses strategic planning and a multi-tiered approach that includes establishing brand recognition, building an image, and developing and launching a major advertising campaign tied into promotional activities and events to support your initial plan. For others, marketing means finding some basic ways to reach your target audience and letting them know what you have to offer.

Most small businesses fall into the latter category and many young entrepreneurs have little time for massive amounts of time and energy expended on marketing plans and preparation.

Earlier we talked about getting to know your target market based on the demographics you've researched and based on the needs in your area. If, for example, there are numerous SAT prep courses in your geographic region, you may not have enough of an available market, meaning you'll need to set your sights in another direction, perhaps tutoring younger students. Once you've zeroed in on whom you are looking to reach, your marketing strategy is essentially determining how, within your budget, you can effectively reach them.

Go to the Source

Where do students have trouble learning? In school. Therefore, you'll want to start by marketing what you do to anyone whom you can talk to in the schools. Since most schools won't align with any one tutoring group (and since some of the teachers are your tutoring competitors), this won't be a formal connection. Instead, you'll need to informally meet and talk with receptive teachers and/or school personnel to get your message across: that you're open for business and can help students in various subjects.

You may be able to post ads on school bulletin boards or even advertise in a school newspaper, depending on the school rules. If they're amenable, have something ready to post on the board or in the paper that highlights your specialties as a tutoring business. You may also find some teachers who would like to work for you as tutors. Guidance counselors are often an excellent contact in the schools. They are rarely competitive tutors, and are typically aware of students who can use the services of a tutor. Remember to market your background and those of your tutors in a succinct, effective manner.

You'll also want to make sure your website is up and running early in your planning process so that you can direct teachers and others to it for more information about your business. Make sure you have your rates and available times posted on your website in advance and on

> **Beware!**
> It may not be easy to get to know teachers and school personnel on their turf. Remember, they're working and you may not belong on school grounds, in a day of heightened security. Be resourceful and find out where teachers go after school lets out. Network in your community. Everyone knows a teacher or two, so use your friends, neighbors, and fellow business owners, and *network*.

any printed literature to avoid miscommunication and misunderstandings in that area.

Posters and Flyers

Looking for some inexpensive, effective means of promoting your business? How about posters and flyers? They're easy to make. Remember the old KISS formula: Keep It Simple and Straightforward. Crowded flyers or posters are hard to read, so spread things out. Consider people reading them when driving or passengers reading your posters from a passing bus.

Also, make sure to proofread posters or flyers very carefully before having them printed. Look for high-traffic areas and make sure you check with business owners to see if you can hand out flyers, leave a pile on the counter, or hang posters. Some will make reciprocal agreements, where you have some means of advertising their business as well.

Teaming Up with Other Businesses

Obviously competing businesses won't be interested in helping you. However, if you're a tutoring and test prep business, you might align yourself with a college planner since you're reaching a similar target group but not in direct competition.

Bookstores and stores where students go for their school supplies are also great places for you to place a poster or a stack of flyers. Again, you can promote the store in your business, either on your website, in your promotion, with a sign in your facility, or by giving some of their promotional items to your tutors to use.

You might also swap discount offers with such a business. A purchase of $20 of school supplies might entitle the bearer to 15 percent off a tutoring sessions. Conversely, each of your students may be entitled to 10 percent off on certain school supplies. Such cooperative agreements can be a fruitful means of marketing.

Word-of-Mouth Marketing

Word-of-mouth marketing can be successful for businesses of any size, especially yours. In fact, it's the leading means of marketing in the tutoring business. Of course today, "word of mouth" includes more than actually "talking" to other people: it also includes texting, IMs, e-mails, and posting content to message boards, which is done by some 32 million people every week.

Tutoring businesses are based on the reputation of their tutors and how successful they are at bringing up the grades and test scores of their students ... and yours is no exception. In addition, tutors who are easy to work with and have a grasp of the needs of the students will generate favorable word of mouth. While good service—meaning quality tutoring—is your best selling point and number-one conversation starter among parents and students, you can enhance word-of-mouth communications by giving people something to talk about.

For example, if students are coming to your facility, provide shealthy, fun snacks, along with bottled water or another beverage. Remember, a little extra not only goes a long way toward drawing people to your business, but also gets people talking, particularly kids who like snacks. You might host an open house for people new to the community. Perhaps an end-of-summer carnival for the kids. It's a promotional gathering and something people, especially kids, will tell their friends about.

A holiday party is a nice gesture, as well. The point is, try to create reasons for people to talk about your tutoring business. Offering little (unique) things can also prompt people to talk. In his book *Word of Mouth Marketing*, author Andy Sernovitz (a word-of-mouth marketing guru) points out that among the many barber shops where you could take your kids for a haircut, one barber shop in Chicago has lines going out the door. Why? Well, for one thing, they give good haircuts. For another, they give the kids toys to play with and offer the dads or moms a cocktail.

A tutoring facility that gives away stuffed animals called a Study Buddy to young learners can generate attention. Silliness and gimmicks can be an inviting way to draw the attention of kids and get them, and their parents, to talk about your tutoring serv-

Successful Word-of-Mouth

Use word-of-mouth marketing by followinging a three-step process.

- Find out where people whom you would like to reach (your target audience) are talking on the internet. Which chat rooms do they go to? What blogs do they read? Which discussion groups are they in? Search and find out where your target market is talking, especially about school and how tough classes are.
- Frequent the areas in which they are talking, not by "jumping in" but instead by listening and learning what's going on. Find out who is doing the talking and what their take is on a subject, and get comfortable with the ongoing communications in the internet community.
- Join in, not as a marketer (they'll kick you right out or call you names), but as someone with something to offer. Build up your credibility and gain their respect.

Once you're accepted, you can refer to your favorite tutoring business.

ice. Remember, a happy youngster who wants to come for tutoring is a prelude to a happy parent ... who will tell other parents how much their child loves tutoring and how much his or her grades have improved. Of course, teenagers are more cynical, but they too can be reached with a focus on what matters to them.

Today, the internet is a marvelous way to generate word-of-mouth marketing. For some businesses an online newsletter, discussed later in the chapter, with forward-to-a-friend links on content of interest can help spread your name around. You can also send information to bloggers who write about education and hope that they will include your business in their blogs. Another option is to respond to blogs, not with advertising (which will be blatant and off-putting) but with comments on the tutoring industry. You can also start your own blog.

Much of your clientele is made up of teens, who spend a tremendous amount of time on the internet, especially on social sites, and IMing each other. If some of your younger tutors or your students mention your business on their sites, that's a major starter for word-of-mouth marketing. Therefore, you need to give them something to talk about: perhaps a contest for the best tutor—who helped you the most and why he or she is the "coolest" tutor. Be creative, and use the right buzzwords to generate attention.

Another excellent option is the old two-for-one coupon or sign up a friend and get 10 percent off. This will encourage people to talk about your business and help bring in more students. While looking for people to talk about you, it's a good idea to focus on those who are talking to your prospective market. Along with teens in chat rooms, you can benefit greatly by getting people who attend PTA (or PTO) meetings and school board meetings, or parents of students in resource rooms. Perhaps you could distribute a 10 percent coupon to PTA (or PTO) members should they want to send their children for tutoring.

Whether you're using coupons and/or bring-a-friend offers, joining in on blogs or in chat rooms, hosting parties or gatherings, or coming up with gimmicks like coolest tutor contests or Study Buddies, you want to find ways to encourage people to talk positively about your business. Of course, as stated in the beginning, high grades and test scores are your best ways of generating talk. Spread your successes around in your marketing (including your website) and by letting people know how your students are doing. People like to talk about success.

Online Newsletters

Online newsletters are offered by numerous businesses, associations, and organizations as a way to maintain ongoing communications with customers and promote what is going on with their businesses. First, you need to make it clear in your literature and on your website that you have a newsletter and that signing up is easy. You should not ask a ton of questions in order for someone to sign up. All you really need is a name and e-mail address. Another non-invasive question or two may be okay, but remember, the more steps involved in signing up, the fewer people will do so.

Once people are on board, you need to have a newsletter ready to send out on a timely schedule, which could be weekly, bi-weekly, monthly, or perhaps bi-monthly. A longer gap than that may not prove effective, as you will lose the sense of continuity. You want people to expect the newsletter every week or two weeks and look forward to it.

The immediate question is: How in the world will you be able to produce a full newsletter in addition to your many other business-related activities? Well, for starters, consider that an online newsletter need not be more than one page, perhaps with links to one or two additional pages. Also consider that stories should be concise and that you can tap into your tutors for story ideas and even ask them to write short articles. You may even gather some material from students, parents, educators, or a local school principal.

The idea is to have content that relates closely to what you do. This could be in the form of tips or lists, as well as actual short (two- or three-paragraph) stories. You might have "10 Great ACT Study Habits" or "How to Set Up the Optimal Homework Location." Stories, lists, and interviews about education, studying, homework, technology (as it relates to students), tests, or other such topics can provide enough interesting content to keep a newsletter going. Internal news about your business should only be included if it affects the students and parents, such as a new location or new courses being offered.

So, how does this help you promote your business? It's easy. Alongside of, and below, your content, you will promote your upcoming courses, your tutoring rates, and your success stories, and even include testimonials.

Combining content with your promotions will keep people reading, since the newsletter will remain fresh, offering something more than just advertising. Additionally, you'll want to include polls, surveys, quizzes, or trivia, as well as a place for feedback. This makes the newsletter interactive. You'll also want to have Forward-to-a-Friend links around key articles.

Finally, when sending an online newsletter, use the same title and

Bright Idea

Make Forward-to-a-Friend part of your online marketing strategy, whether it's for articles on your website or in your newsletter. Forwarding should be easy and take the recipient right to the content, not dump them on a homepage or somewhere else where they need to search for the article. In addition, you might have a space where the sender can add a personal message. This is a great way to let your newsletter subscribers or website visitors draw other subscribers or visitors for you.

"from" line on each issue, which should be the name of your company, so that people know who's sending the e-mail. If you offer more than one newsletter, make sure the name of the newsletter is clearly visible so that the recipient knows which one they're receiving. Perhaps you'll have one for parents and one geared to the students themselves, or you might want to have separate newsletters for high-schoolers and grade-schoolers.

Promotional Items

Hats, t-shirts, sweatshirts, pens, notepads, and other promotional items with the name of your tutoring company can generate attention, especially with a market of students who notice what other students are wearing or carrying around. Focus on trends and go for the look that's currently in vogue. Additionally, see what the kids are buying and perhaps you can come up with an accessory. For students who may not want it immediately known that they're being tutored, you might opt for a logo or a saying that catches someone's attention and starts a conversation. Promotional items can usually be inexpensive when bought in bulk.

In the Committee

Whether you sponsor a baseball team or set up a booth at a county fair or street fair, having a presence in the community is always important and a great low-cost way to promote your business. By getting actively involved in neighborhood events or activities, as well as being omnipresent in business establishments and local associations and community groups, you can make a big splash.

Three Low-Cost Promotional Ideas

1. Write an article on some aspect of education and/or testing and submit it to some of the local newspapers.
2. Offer to speak in the community and the schools on topics about ways to study, retain knowledge, improve your memory, or any areas that will spark some interest and draw a crowd.
3. Offer referral discounts to your current customers.

There are many other possibilities; just energize your creative side and start writing down your own promotional ideas.

Promotional Worksheet

List three promotional ideas that you want to try for your business.

_____

_____

_____

In the Media

The best way to get your tutoring business onto radio, television, and/or websites is to send out press releases about your business. Such releases can include anything from new ways to study or test prep that have proven successful to the high number of students who have worked with your tutors who have gone on to college, to the addition of online tutoring, peer tutoring, or anything that might stand out in your community. Obviously, the more unusual and newsworthy your press release is, the more likely you will attract the attention of editors and producers at radio and television stations, at websites, or for the print media.

Press releases aren't difficult to write and can generate immediate attention for a new business. The goal is to promote your own company news within the short release (typically one to one and a half pages). With a little practice you, too, can write a good press release, and if you visit many business websites (especially those of larger, established companies), you'll find samples in their "press" or "media" sections. You can also check out websites like PR Web (prweb.com) for numerous samples of press releases indexed by industry. Another option is to look at your word processing program. Many software programs, such as Microsoft Office, include press release templates. Use press release templates as a guide while writing your own. Note the ones that draw your attention. You'll immediately see that some get to the point immediately, while others do not "grab" you. Some are written in a reader-friendly manner with easy-to-understand terminology rather than industry jargon.

The key to writing a good press release, especially those that will be sent electronically, is to generate attention with a good headline and a good opening paragraph that succinctly includes the most important aspects of your story. Keep in mind that editors, producers, and freelance writers get numerous press releases and you want your headline and opening paragraph to jump off the page. Don't be cryptic, too subtle, or start off with a long story expecting the reader to keep on going to find the meat of your story. Get to it quickly and make it interesting! Don't try to be too cute, too offbeat, or too mysterious in your message. Yes, you can be clever, but in a manner that doesn't take away from the message or confuse the reader, who will immediately discard the press release or hit delete if he or she is lost.

The headline could be in the form of a question, a statement that reveals part of the news (and piques the reader's attention), a quote, or a statistical fact. Use something that you think will make readers want to read more. Under the headline, you can use a sub-headline that reveals a little more information about your main marketing message or answers the question your headline has posed. The subhead should be used to provide more information that generates additional interest from the readers. Of course, you don't have to have a subhead at all.

The first paragraph needs to grab the reader by making your message sound exciting, without using a lot of "hype." No, your tutors are not the greatest tutors in the world. However, if they have increased SAT scores by an average of 250 points or have created a means of tutoring whereby students can learn by dancing that has proven successful, those make for a headline and an interesting story. Provide the details in a short, to-the-point manner. Use the mindset that you have just seven seconds to wow the reader, because that's about all he or she will spend on a press release unless something strikes a chord.

The second paragraph should provide more details on the story, such as the who, what, where, when, why, and how that can be used by the editor, reporter, producer, or whomever the release is sent to, as a means of fleshing out a story.

Next, you include what is called a boilerplate paragraph, which is essentially a paragraph on your business that can be run on numerous press releases. Keep it to three or four sentences. Lastly, you want to make sure that your contact information is on every page. At the end of a press release, you will usually find the word "end" or ###, a symbol meaning it's over.

Keep in mind that hype and jargon are overused and unnecessary. Dazzle them with what you've accomplished that's newsworthy and not with buzzwords, which anyone can use.

Make sure you have the name of the person at the media source who would be most receptive to an educational story, or perhaps a community story (if you're sponsoring an event or activity) before sending your press releases. You want them in the hands of someone likely to write or assign the story.

Seminars and Conferences

One of the best ways to spread the word about what you have to offer and learn about what your competition is doing, as well as what's going on in the industry, is by attending educational seminars and conferences.

Organizations such as the National Tutoring Association exchange information and present what's new in the field at conferences and gatherings throughout the year. Doing a little searching online and/or joining educational groups and associations can be good ways to learn about and getting involved in such activities and events.

Associations and You

Another good way to network and spread the word about what you do, as well as learn more about your industry, is to become a joiner, and associations are one great place to start. Along with the larger organizations, such as the International, National, and American Tutoring Associations, you may find local associations in your state or region of the country. Why are such organizations of value? Here are seven good reasons to consider getting involved in one, or several, tutoring associations.

- **Knowledge and Updates:** Tutoring associations, as is the case with most associations, are typically up-to-date on the latest industry news and can pass that along to their members through e-mails, newsletters, and meetings or seminars.
- **Conferences:** Many associations hold annual conferences that allow tutors to take part in group discussions, attend workshops, and network all in one place.
- **Websites:** Association websites provide a wealth of current information, and within member sections, often get down to the nitty-gritty in the industry.
- **Networking:** Through meetings, conferences, online discussions, and other interactive technology, associations provide networking possibilities.
- **Referrals:** Many tutoring associations have services for members that let you get the names and profiles of your tutors out to a much larger market.
- **Training and Certification:** Tutoring associations often provide training and certification, such as the online training program and certification offered by ITA.
- **Hiring:** As an entrepreneur, you can find quality tutors by joining a tutoring association and posting a notice that you are in the market for tutors.

Before joining an association, take a look at their website and see what benefits come from signing up. In most cases you'll find that the benefits make the dues or costs worthwhile. From that point on, it's up to you as to how involved you choose to become. Newsletters will alert you to events and activities, so you can pick and choose what interests you. The bottom line is that associations are a good way to learn more about the industry, while also networking and getting your name out there.

A Few Final Tips

If you write your own press releases, make sure to edit and proofread carefully before sending. Remember, spell check doesn't catch everything.

Make sure your contact information is on each page.

If you're hiring a PR company, make sure you find out exactly where your money is going and have them provide reports on what they're doing and how much time it is taking them to do the work. You can also opt for a freelance press release writer; look at his or her work before you hire anyone. A single press release should cost between $50 and $150. This is often a cheaper alternative to expensive PR firms that may lock you in for four months at $2,000 a month.

Save testimonials from satisfied customers. They can be included in press releases, on packaging, in articles you write, and so on.

If you have photos and several press releases, and have generated some print or online stories, you can put together a media kit, which is a collection of all of the above in a nice folder designed with your company name and logo on it. These are costlier to send, but worthwhile for important clients or key potential clients. You may also include a "backgrounder," which is a one-page history of the company.

Advertising

Neal Schwartz of Tutoring Club in Armonk, New York says he's only placed a couple of ads in the four years that he's been in business. He's also done his share of promotional activities, such as having a table each year at the annual town fair.

Advertising means spending money to make money, and it's part of most business agendas. The more wide-reaching your target market, the more likely you'll need to advertise. For example, a tutoring business that has several locations and can accommodate thousands of potential students will be more likely to use advertising than a tutoring business that serves a town of 10,000 people, where word of mouth and some promotional activities can cover the area, as is the case with Neal Schwartz's tutoring club.

Effective advertising means getting the most bang for your buck. Translated, that means reaching the most people in a cost-effective manner. For example, buying an ad in a newspaper for $200 that reaches 100,000 people means you are reaching 500 people for every dollar you spend. If, however, you were to take your ad to local television and spent $3,000 to produce a commercial and $2,000 for advertising time, you would be spending a total of $5,000. If the viewing audience is estimated at 100,000 people, you're only reaching 20 people with each dollar spent.

Of course, there are many other factors to consider. For example, how many people in your target audience read the newspaper? How many people in your target audience watch the television programs on which your ad is running? Some research is necessary to determine the demographics of any potential source of advertising. You'll want to reach parents of school-age children as well as teens and college students. Therefore, you're better off advertising in a local parenting magazine with a circulation of 10,000 potential customers than in a magazine geared for young executives with a circulation of 25,000 read primarily by people who don't yet have kids. The point is, circulation size is not as important as how much of your target audience reads the paper. Most media outlets have demographic information available about their readerships.

You'll need to evaluate the cost factor and how often you can afford to advertise. Keep in mind that effective advertising means repetition so people become familiar with your company name. This way, when a parent feels that his or her child is in need of tutoring or test prep (or a student feels he or she needs some help to do well on the SAT), your business will immediately come to mind.

Other key sources of advertising include:

- Radio (typically not very expensive if ads are purchased in bulk)
- Websites (get the number of visitors and look for sites that fall into your demographics)
- Search engines (pay-per-click advertising is available on Yahoo!, Google and other search engines)
- Signage (this can include signs on buses, taxicabs, etc.)

Content and Parameters

Your ads need to sell your services, whether those include homework help, ongoing tutoring, test prep, or anything else you offer. Of course in limited time or space, you need to go with your strengths and if possible, state what makes your business special or unique. Don't forget your competitive edge!

Advertising can be entertaining to grab attention; however, you want to make sure the message gets through. Too many very clever ads are remembered only for being entertaining, and the viewers can't recall the product or services advertised. You may include graphics in print ads, but keep ads simple and to the point. In web ads, don't try to dazzle people with fancy graphics; again, keep it simple and to the point.

Ads need to be timely. Therefore, if the PSATs are coming up in October, you want to have those ads running by Labor Day to get students signed up in early September for your month-long review course. Of course, an ad running in September needs to be planned in June and the advertising space booked in July. For magazines, there is an even longer lead time. Before advertising anywhere, you need to get the parameters and guidelines of the newspaper, radio station, website, or television station.

- What size ads does the magazine or newspaper offer (quarter-page? half-page? full page?)?
- How much time does a radio or television station offer (15 seconds? 20 seconds? 30 seconds?)?

- How much do they charge for one ad? For several ads?
- When do they need the ad copy?
- Can you record your own radio commercial? Do they offer a recording space? Will an on-air personality read your copy? Will someone help you write the copy?
- Can you do the graphics for a newspaper or photos for a magazine ad, or do they handle it?
- In what section of the newspaper will your ad appear? On what television show? On which page(s) of the website? In what time slot on the radio? On the side of which buses? Know exactly where your ad will be placed and request specific sections, pages, programs, time slots, or bus routes.

These are just some of the many options that you'll have to investigate when you start checking out advertising possibilities.

To advertise, you'll want to have a budget set aside and spread it out so that you can advertise consistently, saving money for specific times of year, such as approaching major exams (SAT, ACT, etc.). You'll also want to establish a consistent look and feel for your ads so there's a recognition factor. A slogan or catchphrase can work wonders. In fact, if you come up with a good one, trademark it.

Advertising: Taking a Look from the Client's Side

Before you spend money to put your ad in the newspaper, on the internet, or anyplace else, it's a good idea to review the ad from the perspective of your clients, that is, the parents of your students or the students themselves. While it may be hard to be objective, you'll want to first determine if the headline would grab your attention in the course of thumbing through a Penny Saver, newspaper, or magazine. Is it simple, and easy to read, such as "SAT Tutoring, Sign Up Now," or is your headline too wordy or complicated? You'll want boldface for your headline and even a larger font if it will fit into the size and space of the ads you want to purchase.

When advertising, remember that ad placement is a factor. If you're lost somewhere among a myriad of ads on a web page, you may be wasting your money. Likewise, you don't want to be in the newspaper section advertising local strip clubs or escort services. Thinking like a customer, you want to place your ads in appropriate places where parents or students would look when seeking educational help.

Then it's a matter of having all of the information that the client is seeking. Can they find answers to the following questions?:

- What subjects does your tutoring business cover?

- Do you offer test prep? If so, is it individual tutoring and/or classes?
- Do you offer tutoring at a facility or at individuals' homes?
- What grade levels are offered?
- If you have a tutoring facility, where is it located and is there parking?
- Are your tutors qualified and/or certified?
- Rates? You may or may not include rates. Often, you'll want to have everything else accounted for and then have them call for your prices, since there may be several options.
- Are there any discounts or special promotions offered?
- Is your contact information included?
- Is the ad clear and easy to read?

Check out the ad below and see if you find the answers to all 10 questions.

TOP GRADES TUTORING SERVICE

Our brand new 20,000-square-foot tutoring facility at 554 Willoughby Street in New Canaan offers K–12 tutoring by certified teachers and tutoring professionals.

Subjects include math, English, science, world and American history, Spanish, French, Italian, and German. Special introductory reading classes are offered by certified reading specialists.

Test Prep classes are also offered for the PSAT, SAT, and ACT.

Call 1-800-xxx-xxxx for a free consultation. Plenty of free parking.

Visit our website at topgrades.com.

Sign up for SAT Prep courses before September 5th and save 15%!

Now it's your turn. Here's a sample ad form. You can move and manipulate the order of the information when do your actual layout. In the meantime, use the form to cover your advertising needs:

Headline:

Location or home tutoring offered:

Age range:

Subjects:

Test prep:

Tutor qualifications:

Rates, or how you want to address them:

Special offers:

Parking, if applicable, or mass transit (e.g., one block from the Tompkins Street Subway station: the E or F trains)

Contact information:

In the above ad, a brand-new 20,000-square-foot facility is mentioned as a selling point. If you have any such selling point, include it, such as new teaching technology or free pick-up and drop-off within a two-mile radius (meaning you'll need a bonded driver and a vehicle), which is uncommon, but a possibility if the client is close.

15 Advertising and Marketing Recommendations

1. Try to use any relationships you have with teachers. Ask them if they can recommend your services.
2. Put up posters and hand out flyers wherever possible. This is an inexpensive means of spreading the word about your business.
3. Use the local Penny Saver. This is a form of inexpensive advertising that you can run often.
4. Post your tutoring on local bulletin boards in libraries, stores, laundromats, etc. (make sure you have permission to do so).
5. If your tutors are certified, or you're working with licensed teachers, include that in your advertising.
6. If you specialize in certain subjects or specific tests, mention them in your ads and other marketing materials.
7. Try to advertise in conjunction with local stores that sell school supplies and/or school books, since your target audience will be shopping at these locations.
8. Promote your services to homeschool groups, since homeschooling is becoming more common today.
9. Look for speaking opportunities to talk about educational trends, testing, competition for college, and other subjects of interest to parents and students in your community. This is a great source of free publicity.
10. Offer yourself as an expert in education for the local media. This way you can be quoted in print stories or appear on interviews for radio or television (or even online).

11. Get to know the people in the local school district offices so that they can refer students to your business.
12. Get to know people in the business community, such as the local chamber of commerce. They have children in the local school system.
13. Build relationships with private school teachers and administrators.
14. Talk to parents in community groups about education and your services.
15. Join online discussion groups and work your way into chats or interactive online areas in which you can contribute. Don't blatantly advertise, however, or you'll lose people's interest. This is not the forum for such advertising, but a place to simply get the word out.

Monitor Your Advertising

The last important aspect of your advertising plan should be to find out where people are hearing about your business. You'll want to ask parents and/or students how they found out about your business. Perhaps a survey card can do this for you, asking if they heard about you through:

- Flyers
- Posters
- Word-of-mouth
- Their child's school
- Newspaper ad
- Other _____

Include all possible ways in which you have promoted or advertised yourself. Always include word of mouth, which, as you've read, is a leading means of generating business for tutoring companies. In fact, this multi-billion-dollar industry is fueled by word of mouth.

Tracking the responses to your advertising and promotional efforts will allow you to allocate money accordingly for your next round of ads and promotional activities. As many tutoring business owners have found, you can do well with minimal, yet well placed, local ads along with a series of promotional activities, a good website, and a plan to start and sustain word-of-mouth marketing.

Your Sales
Strategy

Any successful business needs a means of selling their products or services. In the tutoring and test prep business, that means selling either based on your hourly tutoring rates or a specific test prep course. While advertising and marketing draw customers to your business, it is up to you, with the help of your tutors, to close the deal.

Sales Options

Since tutoring is rarely a one-time activity, you're selling a series of sessions over a specific period of time. Many tutoring facilities, like Neal Schwartz's Tutoring Club, set up an ongoing time slot for the student and tutor to meet and maintain that as a regular session with no formal agreement. If the student (or tutor) cannot make a session, there is no payment and the session is rescheduled only if there is a mutual time available for student and tutor or another tutor fills in. For many tutoring facilities, such a casual format works because of the ongoing need for tutoring. Not unlike physical therapy, students and parents see the value of the tutoring sessions and keep coming back.

Selling this type of tutoring means selling one tutoring session and then promoting on the value of such a session on a regular basis. The onus is on the tutor to make the initial session worthwhile and demonstrate what he or she can do. This is where the value of the sales opportunity comes into focus. As a business owner, you need to stress to your tutors that they not only have to do a good job as a tutor, but make it clear that the next session will move the process forward. A reading tutor working with youngsters might say, "Next time we'll try sounding out two-syllable words," or a math or science tutor might explain that having become comfortable with the basic concepts or formulas, the student will be able to use them next time. By selling the idea that there is more work to be done, you show the student and parent that there is an ongoing plan and a reason to keep returning. Obviously this winds down at the end of the semester.

"We have a lot of students coming in over the summer to gear up for the upcoming year," says Schwartz, who was initially surprised by the number of students who were ready and willing to work during part of their vacation.

Another option is to have a contract for x number of tutoring sessions that can be expanded.. This makes cash flow a bit easier, since you collect payment up front, or at least a portion of it, and your tutor and student have a set time frame in which to work. Again, there may be a need for occasional rescheduling.

As is typically the case in sales, some people will not want to be "locked into a set number of sessions," while others will feel a stronger connection. People constantly sign up for 10 yoga classes or 12 visits to the gym. Therefore, if they are comfortable with your offering and your rates, this can be a way to secure steady business. You may have one low-priced session as a lead-in to the 10- or 20-session plan. You may also offer both options, with a discount for the contracted plan. For example, if you charge $65 for an hour of tutoring, you could offer 20 sessions for $1,000, which is $50 each.

Draw up a simple agreement for clients to sign for multiple classes. Anything with numerous clauses or lots of detail will be off-putting. Remember, paying for x amount of hours over x amount of weeks is not a complicated process. Work on such an agreement with your attorney.

You'll also want to have an agreement ready for signing up students for your test prep courses. Selling such courses today is based largely on the notion that "everyone is looking to get an edge, so why shouldn't you?" While you may agree that the competition to get into colleges today has gone a bit overboard, as a business owner it's not your job to refute or fight the system. The SAT and the ACT have gained significant status, and the best you can do is sell the fact that you offer a way to help students improve their chances of doing well on these important exams.

Selling test prep courses means starting your campaign well in advance of the tests and even offering discounts for early sign-up. Since clients are starting to shy away from large classes because of poor reviews, you can offer a series of smaller-sized classes. Remember, with these exams, students can also take them more than once. This allows you to continue selling the courses to the same students with an emphasis on "doing better" the next time. A good test prep course is fueled largely by the success of its students. Therefore, it's an important part of your sales strategy to get as many of the scores from your previous students as possible. The higher their scores, the more sales ammunition you have.

Of course, there's an art to selling and landing a client. No, you cannot use the old "used car sales tactics" whereby you tell the buyer anything he or she wants to hear. Your job is to make the parents feel that you can help their child improve, whether it means getting their homework done correctly, their grades improved, and/or better test results.

Selling a service is largely about:

- Solving a problem
- Self-improvement
- Comfort

You go to a dentist because he or she can make your tooth stop hurting (solving a problem). You want whiter teeth (self-improvement). You look for a dentist who is gentle and instills confidence that you're in good hands (comfort).

Likewise, you want to emphasize that your tutors can help the child do better in school (solving a problem). Your tutors will teach better methods for the student to improve on his or her own (self-improvement). Your tutors are skilled, certified, flexible, likable, personable, etc. (they make the parent and student feel comfortable).

These are the points you want to get across when selling your tutoring, along with personalized attention, since no two student–tutor relationships will be identical.

Meet the Parents:
Selling to Your Real Clients

Prior to commencing a tutor–student relationship, you'll have an initial consultation with the parents (unless you're dealing with older students coming from college or postgraduate courses on their own).

As an entrepreneur, you need to look at this as an opportunity to sell your services to clients. Since your service is tutoring, the key is to find a match that puts one of your tutors with the client's son or daughter in order to facilitate and enhance the learning experience in one or several subject areas.

You want to know:

- Why is the client there? (How can I help you?)

- What grade level is the student? (Don't guess. If you look at a child and say he's probably in fifth grade and he's in seventh, you can be sure that kid won't come back.)

- In which areas is the student struggling? (In what subjects is he/she having difficulty?)

- What academic history does the student have? (What grades does he/she typically get?)

Typically, you will get the answers to all these questions with the initial "How can I help you?"

Once the parent has provided the essentials, it's always worthwhile to get the student involved in the conversation in a non-threatening, friendly manner. Judging by the body language and expression of the child, you can usually tell if he or she was dragged in or was brought to tutoring with a mutual understanding that the tutor can be a helper and it's okay to get some help. Either way, almost all kids can think of more fun things to do with their time than go to tutoring. Therefore, you want to make the experience as painless as possible while also selling the parent on the idea that something will get accomplished and that their child is in good hands.

You can do this by balancing the credentials of your tutors and their experience with a fun non-school-like atmosphere and tutors who really are "great to work with." Let the student know that he or she will really like the tutor, and in fact, if you strike up a conversation with the student about what he or she likes (hobbies, interests), you can usually find some common ground. "Jerry's also a big hockey fan," or "You'll get along great with Carolyn, she's also a karaoke singer." As soon as the tutor becomes less "teacher" and more "human" in the eyes of the student, his or her anxiety will begin to subside. And, as soon as you assure the parent(s)/client(s) that the tutor is excellent in the subject area, you're on the way to a sale.

Money is the next area of concern. This, however, is one in which you will want to be firm yet flexible within reason. If, for example, someone is unsure if they can sign up for 20 weeks, then go to your 10-week plan and let them know that they can see how it goes after that. Of course, you can always upsell if you know the testing schedule. For example, "We can start off with 10 weeks of tutoring, and then if you feel in December he may need more help with midterms coming up, we can do another 10 weeks around that time."

Always stay a little bit ahead of the current needs of your clients. The school year is long and neither parents nor students may want to commit for the entire year, especially if mom or dad is driving back and forth to your tutoring facility. However, as the year goes along, there will be more and more reasons (midterms, state tests, finals, etc.) to keep the relationship going.

Let the parents know that your door is always open for questions or concerns and that you'll be watching over the tutoring—which you need to do with all your students through ongoing meetings with your tutors.

Make sure you schedule these introductory meetings, or consultations, at times when you can devote your full attention to the new clients and aren't in the middle of numerous other things. You lose a lot of credibility if it appears that you are disorganized.

How do You Keep Your Customers?

Every six or 12 months, you often get a postcard from your dentist or eye doctor reminding you to return for a check-up. Well, since school pretty much dictates the schedule for you, it's to your benefit to get those cards and e-mails out to your clients shortly before the school year kicks off. Being aware of midterms, finals, and statewide tests, along with the SAT and ACT schedules, gives you the opportunity to reach out to customers with well-timed reminders to sign up now.

Maintaining your customer base is vital to any business. The old 80–20 philosophy holds true for service businesses such as yours. That's where 80 percent of your business will come from 20 percent of your customers. Therefore, once you've established that your tutoring meets the needs of a middle schooler or grade schooler, you can be there for the student right up through high school, or beyond if and when he or she needs your help. And don't forget about brothers and sisters.

Attention to detail plays a major role in retaining customers in a service-based business. Knowing not only the students' names, but the parents' names as well and having some basic data on your clients goes a long way. A birthday card is a small price to pay to let them know that they're part of your tutoring family. Following the school path and (hopefully) success of a student as he or she moves through school is part of building your relationship. And, after all, maintaining regular customers is all about establishing and nurturing those relationships.

▲

Together with your tutors, you'll want to build a sense of trust so that parents feel comfortable calling on you when their children need help, but also letting you know when things are going well. Often parents will stop sending a child to tutoring for a while, either for financial reasons or simply because they feel their son or daughter is doing well enough and doesn't need to keep on coming. In some cases, the child may simply have a busy schedule between school and extracurricular activities. It's not at all uncommon for this to occur. Often, they will return when final exams loom on the horizon or it's PSAT and SAT time. For that reason, you maintain your database and never simply delete someone because they haven't shown up for a few months. Until the parents are empty nesters, you need to have that family in your files for ongoing mailings or e-mails, just like the eye doctor and dentist. Keep them abreast of new courses you have and let them know you're thinking about them as long as the family has someone in the school system.

Bright Idea

Actually, this is beyond a bright idea—it's a must for any business today. Back up your computer data files! Whether you contact an offsite data backup and storage facility, or you copy everything onto a CD or flash drive and store it in your safety deposit vault, Make sure that you have some sort of data backup storage updated so that you're never more than one week behind. Hurricanes like Katrina and Rita made it abundantly clear how quickly businesses can lose their power and in some cases, be wiped out. Flash floods, tornados, and fires occur. From a business standpoint, you need to be ready to reopen with your data saved and accessible. Having offsite backup data is essential today for any business.

Expanding Your Business: Additional Sales Opportunities

As a business owner, you can seek out additional sources of revenue from products and services related to your business. In the next chapter, we'll discuss additional types of services you can offer. Here, we can examine the possibility of promoting and selling products that can add to your bottom line. You may offer written materials and/or CDs that complement the course work, as well as appropriate books and workbooks.

Knowing the school curriculum and having a feel for the needs of your students from interacting with your individual tutors, you can determine which educational products, if any, could be additional sales items.

Some learning specialists, which may include your own tutors, have created books for youngsters learning to read or other materials that can benefit students. In this case, you can work out a deal with the author to either help with the publishing of the book and split the profits or, if it's already published, provide marketing and promotion for an agreed-on percentage of the sales price. Whatever you agree on, have a signed contract so that both you and your tutor or "specialist" know what to expect when it comes to future proceeds.

If you have the time, you may be able to create your own work/study guides that you can sell as accompanying materials to the course work or to the test prep guides. Rather than focusing on the materials found in already-published books, you might opt instead for a broad guide to studying, a homework helper, or another type of general book that you can sell at a low price to cover the printing and provide a little profit.

The idea of expanding your lines of revenue is to make more money without taking away from the time that you need to put into the business and without spending much of your profits. Start small and see if there's a demand for such books, workbooks, CDs, software, or related materials. To save on inventory and printing, you might even make some low-cost items available in electronic form from your website.

Additional Revenue

From books to backpacks, you can create another source of revenue through sales. The key to success in this area, however, is buying in enough quantity to make some profit, while not pricing items higher than local stores. This means having some space available for inventory.

If you do find a trustworthy wholesaler and get a good price on school supplies, this can become another source of income. Be careful, however, not to lose sight of your primary objective(s) as a tutoring and test prep business.

13

Other
Offerings

Today there are many specialties in every industry. The tutoring and test prep business is no exception. Since education is such a broad field, your business can spill over into offering other services and providing access to other professionals who provide the necessary services.

Among the many possibilities, we list four distinct and important areas you might consider adding to your business:

- Reading specialists for young children
- College planning specialists and/or consultants for high school students
- ESL teachers for people from around the world now living in America
- Career training for individuals entering (or already in) the work force

Each of these, as well as other specific areas, can be another source of revenue for your business. Just make sure you do your research to see if there's a need in your community and, if there is such a need, promote such added services accordingly. Also, make sure to hire qualified experts in these fields with the necessary experience to enhance your reputation.

Reading Specialists

Reading specialists play an important role for the many young children who struggle with reading. Nearly every school today has a reading specialist on staff or easily accessible. However, as the demand for extra reading help grows, many parents are looking beyond the school for someone who can devote more time to their child's needs. Your business can offer a reading specialist who can work on a one-on-one basis with young readers. Such a specialist will assess each child's specific reading problems, keeping in mind that in some cases they may be related to visual problems or perceptual problems.

Busy working parents today are not always able to read with their children daily, and that can be a common source of problems as the child does not become familiar with the reading process. A reading specialist can work with phonetics, address trouble areas, and use any of a great number of techniques at their disposal to help children learn how to read and comprehend material. A good reading specialist has patience and is attentive, picking up on common errors made by the child and making corrections while building the child's confidence.

What you can offer such a specialist, besides a place in which to work with young readers, is promotion and advertising. Once word gets around that you offer specific reading help, you will very likely see a quick and positive response, with plenty of parents signing up.

College Advistors

Before discussing the notion of having a college advisor, planner, or consultant as part of your business, or accessible through your business, let's discuss your ability to offer some general college information to high school students and their parents.

There are 4,100+ colleges and universities throughout the United States. If you're tutoring high school students, having some general knowledge of what it takes to get into these schools is a major plus for your business. College advisors, planners, and consultants are part of a separate industry. However, tapping into some of that knowledge can be beneficial. You'll want to have information available on acceptance standards, programs offered, and campus life for some of the most popular and/or most prominent schools. While you don't want to pose as an expert in the field, you should be able to answer some of the basic questions.

Along with data on the Ivy League schools and other leading universities from an academic perspective, you should also have some information available on the top state schools in whichever state(s) your business resides. Also, take some time to pay a visit to the local colleges, including community colleges, and learn what you can about their programs, courses, costs, and so on. Being able to provide some assistance to a wider range of students is valuable and another means of generating a "buzz" about your business.

For more precise information and guidance, you can also point students and parents in the direction of full-time planners, advisors, and consultants. Most professionals in the field have previously worked as teachers, professors, or directors of admissions, or held other educational positions, typically at the university level.

If you choose to hire a specialist in a college advisory role, or tread that water yourself, offering some assistance to those who can't afford the full-scale college consultant, you'll want to provide information in the following areas:

- The college selection process for students
- Criteria for the colleges (what they are looking for from students)
- Test requirements and percentiles for getting accepted
- Admissions policies
- The flavor, reputation, and atmosphere of various schools
- Costs
- Qualifications for any financial assistance

Providing assistance and information in these areas means doing a lot of research, visiting colleges, and reading as much as you can find on the schools. It also helps to meet with people

Bright Idea

One way to add to your bottom line is by offering seminars, webinars (online seminars), and lectures. Once you're confident that you know your target audience, you can select a few topics of interest and plan some inexpensive special events featuring some of your tutors. Such offerings can help:
- Promote your business
- Bring in additional revenue
- Spotlight a tutor's strength and special knowledge in an area

involved in the admissions programs for a wide range of universities. Don't have time to do all of this? In that case, you can have some general answers to meet the needs of students in these areas, and then turn to the professional college advisors, planners, and consultants to do their jobs. Building an alliance with such a planner, consultant, or advisor can be a productive and beneficial partnership for both sides.

English as a Second Language

Another offering that has been introduced into numerous learning centers is English as a second language. The vast diversity among people in the United States has created an increasing need for ESL courses and, in some cases, private tutoring. Before offering such courses, however, it's always recommended that you do your research to determine if there's a need for ESL classes in your community, or whether there is room for another ESL course, if several are already available.

If you decide that you would like to offer an ESL class, you'll first want to seek out and hire ESL instructor with experience. You may seek out someone with a master's degree in Teaching English as a Second or Other Language (TESOL).

Based on the target market, it's likely that you'll want to schedule classes for evenings and/or weekend hours. You'll also need to determine if you'll offer beginner, intermediate or advanced classes, or all three. As is the case with any class offerings, you may want to offer choices, and you will need to secure space for such a class. If you have your own facility, this shouldn't be a problem. If not, you'll be looking for a space to accommodate your needs, which will likely include a whiteboard and possibly slides of other technical aspects.

Next, if you come from an education background, you'll want to work with your ESL teacher(s) to make sure you have a program designed and in place prior to starting classes. Depending on the age level and the goals of your class, you can decide on appropriate books, audio recordings, other materials, and lesson plans for students. If you're not from a teaching background, you may need to give your ESL teacher(s) greater leeway in creating a plan of action. In any case, you'll want to have them present it so that you're aware of the types of materials to be used and lessons that will be taught. In an effort not to recreate the wheel, you can also guide your teacher(s) to websites with lesson plans for ESL students. For example, About.com: English as a Second Language offers numerous lesson plans for beginner, intermediate, and advanced levels.

Programs and lesson plans will focus on teaching only English speaking and reading, or include writing or additional areas, such as business reading and writing. Once again, your research and knowledge of what is most in demand will factor into the decision as to what your class(es) will include.

For greater insight into the world of ESL, you can visit TESOL, the international organization for ESL/EFL teachers (with over 20,000 members), online at tesol.edu, or call (703) 836-0774.

In addition to hiring the most qualified ESL teacher(s) and making sure that lesson plans are created in line with the areas you wish to offer (e.g., reading, speaking, etc.) you'll want to have books and CDs available. Numerous sources, such as Language Success Press (languagesuccesspress.com) or Alta Books (altaesl.com) have a number of books available—ask for a catalog. You'll also find ESL books from large publishing houses such as Oxford University Press or Addison-Wesley. Make sure to match the level of the books and other materials to the levels of your students.

Finally, you need to have clear goals in sight. What level of progress do you expect from your ESL students? Can you gauge how much they should be able to learn in x number of classes? This will take some research and, again, in an effort not to reinvent the wheel, you can look at classes that are offered elsewhere, and, if possible, find individuals who have taken ESL classes and ask them about the experience. You might hold a focus group, bringing together people who have taken ESL classes for a $50 honorium and/or

> **Bright Idea**
> Go with some fun and games. Popular lesson plans for ESL students are "games" which might include spelling or phonics games, finding words, or vocabulary games. Making ESL fun is a great way to hold the attention of your students and achieve success.

dinner, to review your class offering and find out if they believe it would help others like themselves learn English. Such marketing can put you on the right track when planning these classes. In the end, you want to be able to promote an ESL class with the confidence that students should walk away with the ability to speak, read, and/or write the English language at some level of proficiency.

Career Advancement and Training

Almost every industry today requires some degree of specialized training to move up the ladder. In addition to your tutoring and test prep business, you can also offer career advancement classes and test preparation in any of numerous fields.

By researching your geographic area and determining some of the fastest-growing industries, you can design your career training program to cover the most current business and professional needs. Whether you're training recent graduates who are entering new fields, individuals seeking a career change, or the many hard workers who are looking for career advancement within their industry, you can offer the classes and even accreditation by meeting the necessary standards and industry requirements.

▲

Among the numerous possibilities for courses and/or training sessions or seminars are:

Business courses, including:

- Account management
- Advertising
- Crisis management
- Entrepreneurship
- Human resources
- Managing people
- Marketing
- Project management
- Supply chain management

Sales courses, including:

- Closing sales
- Customer services
- Prospecting
- Retail sales strategies
- Sales techniques

Computer courses, including:

- Computer analysis
- IT certification courses
- Microsoft courses, including systems administration, certification prep, etc.
- Offsite data backup
- Networks and networking
- Programming
- Software design
- Software management
- Troubleshooting
- Web design

Real estate courses, including:

- Appraisals
- Broker certification courses
- Home inspection
- Real estate licensing

Obviously, these are just a few of the multitude of possibilities. The point is, you can branch out and train people in a variety of fields with qualified instructors. From automobile detailing to restaurant management to licensing courses for a masseuse or training for registered nurses prior to taking the nursing exam, you can provide the skills necessary.

Such professional courses and/or training programs will typically require you to

Such professional courses and/or training programs will typically require you to have adequate space for a class and available evening hours. If you are running a tutoring service from a home base, you can rent out a larger facility on an ongoing basis to run the training courses. Look at schools, libraries, hotels, and community centers for evening availability. Then price your training competitively based on the going rates for training programs in the industry.

If you go this route, make sure to market not only the courses, but also any certificates that you can provide (legally) and the credentials of the instructor(s).

Now and in the Future

For most entrepreneurs starting a tutoring and test prep business, offerings such as those mentioned in this chapter may be a little farther down the road. The reason they are mentioned here is that it's always important to think ahead and consider ways you can grow and build your business.

There is a need to support and encourage education at all levels and in numerous ways, whether it's helping a child learn to read or assisting a senior as he or she finds a career path and perhaps opens a business of his or her own. Schools today are very competitive from the grade school years up through postgraduate and business schools. The working environment also provides greater challenges than ever before, with extreme competition to move up the ladder. For these reasons, the tutoring, test prep, and career advancement industries are growing rapidly, and you can be a part of this world by carefully developing and building such additional business resources. It has long been said that for a business to do well, it must keep moving forward with new ideas, new products, and new services.

And in the End

Starting a tutoring and test prep business is not difficult. Making it work, among many similar businesses and with numerous freelance tutors out there is another story. For that reason, you need to plan carefully and strategically. By studying the industry, analyzing the competition, evaluating the possible approaches, writing a business plan, hiring highly qualified tutors, and strategically marketing your business, you can build a successful business. By carefully watching your expenses, your reputation and your bottom line, you can maintain such a business. And, by seeking new options, new opportunities and staying on top of the latest in trends and technology, you can build your business into a major player in the industry.

141

Appendix:
Tutoring
Resources

Associations

American Educational Resource Association
aera.net
1430 K St. NW, Ste. 1200
Washington, DC 20005
(202) 238-3200

American Tutoring Association
americantutoringassociation.org
(800) 834-3604
Association for the Advancement of Computing in Education
aace.org
PO Box 1545
Chesapeake, VA 23327-1545
(757) 366-5606

Association for Educational Communications and Technology
aect.org

1800 N. Stonelake Dr., Ste. 2
Bloomington, IN 47404
(877) 677-AECT

Association for the Tutoring Professional
atp.jsu.edu/
East Stroudsburg University
Association for the Tutoring Professional
200 Prospect St.
East Stroudsburg, PA 18301-2999

Association of Colleges for Tutoring & Learning Assistance
actla.info
Center for the Integration of Research, Teaching, and Learning
cirtl.net
1025 W. Johnson St., Ste. 552
Madison, WI 53706
(608) 263-0630

College Reading & Learning Association
crla.net.
Distance Education & Training Council
detc.org
1601 18th St., NW, Ste. 2
Washington, DC 20009
(202) 234-5100

Educational Testing Service
ets.org
Rosedale Rd.
Princeton, NJ 08541
(609) 921-9000

International Reading Association
reading.org
800 Barksdale Rd.
PO Box 8139
Newark, DE 19714-8139
(800) 336-7323

International Society for Performance Improvement
ispi.org
1400 Spring St., Ste. 260
Silver Spring, MD 20910
(301) 587-8570

International Tutoring Association
itatutor.org
(909) 266-8595

Law School Administration Council
lsat.org
662 Penn St.
Newtown, PA 18940
(215) 968-1001

National Association for Developmental Education
500 N. Estrella Pkwy.
Ste. B2 PMB 412
Goodyear, AZ 85338
(877) 233-9455

National College Testing Association
ncta-testing.org
National Tutoring Association
ntatutor.com
PO Box 6840
Lakeland, FL 33807-6840
(863) 529-5206

Textbook and/or Test Publishing Houses

ABDO Publishing Company
Grades K–12
abdopub.com
8000 W. 78th St., Ste. 310
Edina, MN 55439
(800) 800-1312

Cengage Learning, Inc.
cenage.com
(formerly Thomson Learning, imprints include Brookes/Cole, Delmar, South-Western, Wadsworth, and others)
PO Box 6904
Florence, KY 41022-6904
(800) 354-9706

College Board
collegeboard.com
SAT review books
45 Columbus Ave.

New York, NY 10023-6917

EMC Paradigm
emcp.com
875 Montreal Way
St. Paul, MN 55102
(800) 535-6865

Harcourt
harcourt.com
(includes four divisions covering all levels of school plus Corporate and Professional services)
6277 Sea Harbor Dr.
Orlando, FL 32887
(407) 345-2000

Houghton Mifflin Company
(divisions include school, college, reference, trade, and others)
hmco.com
222 Berkeley St.
Boston, MA 02116
(617) 351-5000

Jones and Bartlett Publishers
jbpub.com
40 Tall Pine Dr.
Sudbury, MA 01776
(800) 832-0034

Kaplan Test Prep & Admissions
(includes the popular SAT and ACT review guides)
kaptest.com
1-800-KAP-TEST

The McGraw-Hill Companies
mcgraw-hill.com
PO Box 182604
Columbus, OH 43272
(800) 262-4729

Pearson Education
pearsoned.com
(imprints and divisions include Addison-Wesley, Prentice Hall, and Scott Foresman Publishing, among others)
One Lake St.
Upper Saddle River, NJ 07458
(201) 236-7000

The Princeton Review
princetonreview.com
(numerous test review books)

W. W. Norton & Company, Inc.
wwnorton.com
500 Fifth Ave.
New York, NY 10110
(212) 354-5500

Tutoring Franchises

Club Z!
clubz.com
15310 Amberly Dr., #185
Tampa, FL 33647
(800) 434-2582

***Entrepreneur* Magazine (Top 500 Franchises, annual list)**
entrepreneur.com/franchise500
Entrepreneur Media Inc.
2445 McCabe Way, Ste. 400
Irvine, CA 92614
(949) 261-2325

Franchise Business Review
(reviews franchises)
franchisebusinessreview.com
3 Badgers Island W.
Kittery, ME 03904
(866) 397-6680

Huntington Learning Centers, Inc.
huntingtonlearning.com
496 Kinderkamack Rd.
Oradell, NJ 07649
(800) 653-8400 / (201) 261-8400

Sylvan Learning Centers
sylvanlearning.com
1001 Fleet St.
Baltimore, MD 21202
(800) 284-8214 / (410) 843-8000

Tutoring Club LLC
tutoringclub.com

11241 Eastern Ave.
Henderson, NV 89052
(888) 674-6425 / (702) 588-5288

U.S. Government Agencies and Business Associations

Internal Revenue Service (IRS)
(all federal and business tax information, directly from the source)
irs.gov
111 Constitution Ave., NW
Washington, DC 20224
800-829-4933

National Small Business Association (NSBA)
(a volunteer-based agency, focusing on small business advocacy in an effort to promote federal policies of benefit to small businesses and the growth of free enterprise. Since 1937, the NSBA has grown from representing 160 small businesses to representing over 150,000)
nsba.biz
1156 15th St. NW, Ste. 1100
Washington, DC 20005
800-345-6728

Service Corps of Retired Executives (SCORE)
(a nonprofit association in partnership with the SBA to provide aspiring entrepreneurs and business owners with free business counseling and mentoring programs. The association consists of more than 11,000 volunteer business counselors in 389 regional chapters throughout the United States)
score.org
409 Third St., SW, 6th Fl.
Washington, DC 20024
(800) 634-0245

SBA
(provides new entrepreneurs and existing business owners with financial, technical, and management resources to start, operate, and grow a business. To find the local SBA office in your region log onto sba.gov/regions/states.html)
sba.gov
409 3rd St., SW
Washington, DC 20416
(800) 827-5722

U.S. Association for Small Businesses and Entrepreneurs
(an affiliate of the International Council for Small Business, the USASBE is estab-

lished to advance knowledge and business education through seminars, conferences, white papers, and programs)
usasbe.org/index.asp
UW–Madison
Grainger Hall
975 University Ave., #3260
Madison, WI 53706
(608) 262-9982

U.S. Census Bureau
(demographics available in numerous categories have made up the U.S. Census since 1790 and can be a source of demographic information for developing your target market)
census.gov

U.S. Chamber of Commerce
(represents small businesses, corporations, and trade associations from coast to coast)
uschamber.com
1615 H St., NW
Washington, DC 20062-2000
(800) 638-6582 / (202) 659-6000

U.S. Department of Labor–Office of Small Business Programs
(promotes opportunities for small businesses, including small disadvantaged businesses, women-owned small businesses, HUBZone businesses, and businesses owned by service-disabled veterans)
dol.gov/osbp
Frances Perkins Building
200 Constitution Ave., NW
Washington, DC 20210
(866) 4-USA-DOL

Business Magazines

Barron's
barrons.com
200 Liberty St.
New York, NY 10281
(800) 369-2834

Business Week
businessweek.com
The McGraw-Hill Companies

▲

PO Box 182604
Columbus, OH 43272
(877) 833-5524

Entrepreneur **magazine**
entrepreneur.com
Entrepreneur Media Inc.
2445 McCabe Way
Irvine, CA 92614
(800) 274-6229

Forbes
forbes.com
90 5th Ave.
New York, NY 10011
(800) 295-0893

Franchise Times
franchisetimes.com
2808 Anthony Lane S.
Minneapolis, MN 55418
(800) 528-3296

Tutoring Books

While there are a number of books on "how to tutor," the bulk of those available were written upward of 10 years ago, prior to the surge in tutoring or the modern technology used today. Here are a few of the more recent entries.

500 Tips for Tutors by Phil Race, Routledge Falmer; 2nd edition (December 2004)

A Parent's Guide to Tutors and Tutoring: How to Support the Unique Needs of Your Child by James Mendelsohn, Jossey-Bass (September 2008)

Peer Tutoring: A Teacher's Resource Guide by Edward E. Gordon, Scarecrow Education (March 2005)

The Tutoring Revolution: Applying Research for Best Practices, Policy Implications, and Student Achievement by Edward E. Gordon, Rowman & Littlefield Education (November 2006)

Software

Along with the software products featured here, these companies typically offer other software applications that may also be beneficial to your business.

Accounting Tools for Tutors

Home Tutoring Business

accountingtoolsfortutors.com

AVG Antivirus and AVG Internet Security
AVG Technologies
grisoft.com
Bit Defender Security 2009
Bit Defender
bitdefender.com

Blackboard Software
blackboard.com
Business Plan Pro
Palo Alto Software
paloalto.com

Groupboard Software
(whiteboards)
groupboard.com
Internet Security 2008

Trend Micro (makers of PC-cillin)
trendmicro.com
Marketing Plan Pro
Palo Alto Software
paloalto.com

McAfee Virus
McAfee
mcafee.com
Microsoft Money, Office, Small Business Accounting, Windows, MSN, etc.
Microsoft
microsoft.com

Norton AntiVirus 2008
Symantec
symantec.com

Panda Antivirus
Interactive Brands
antivirus-08.com

Quicken, QuickBooks, and TurboTax Software
Intuit
intuit.com

Schedule It Pro 4
Schedule It software
scheduleit.co.uk

TimeSheet
Dovico Software
dovico.com

When to Work
whentowork.com

Credit Bureaus

Equifax
equifax.com
(800) 685-1111

Experian
experian.com
(888) 397-3742

Transunion
transunion.com
(800) 916-8800

Index

Index